A Little Book of
Candle Magic

D. J. Conway

THE CROSSING PRESS

The Crossing Press
www.crossingpress.com

A division of Ten Speed Press
P.O. Box 7123
Berkeley, California 94707
www.tenspeed.com

Library of Congress Cataloging-in-Publication Data

Conway, D. J. (Deanna J.)
    A little book of candle magic / by D. J. Conway.
        p. cm.
    Includes bibliographical references and index.
    ISBN 1-58091-043-2 (pbk.)
    1. Candles and lights—Miscellania 2. Magic. I. Title.
    BF1623.C26 C66   2000
    133'.2—dc21   99-057495
                                                            CIP

First printing, 2000
Printed in the U.S.A.

5 6 7 8 9 10 — 06 05 04 03 02

Contents

CHAPTER 1

Candles and Fire
in Religious History

Humankind has always held a deep respect for fire and its power. This respect for and curiosity about fire probably began when humans first became brave enough to take fires caused by lightning back to their camping places to use for warmth and cooking. Some archaeologists place this occurring about 250,000 to 500,000 years ago. Until humans learned how to start fires on their own, these early people were very careful to keep such "captured, sacred" fire burning at all times.

It was not long before humans discovered that fire had two aspects: the sacred and the mundane. Shamans kindled their fires in specific ways with special woods. They used this fire to light mysterious caves and sacred power sites that only certain people entered for mystical rituals. These holy fires helped the shaman and other initiated participants connect with the spiritual worlds where they received messages and first learned healing and magic. Later, they learned other secrets, such as metalworking.

Because fire could be either creative or destructive, those who handled fire were considered to be divinely touched.

Early myths and legends tell of various divine beings who either stole fire from heaven, as Prometheus did, or who gave this wonderful gift to humans so they could survive and worship the deities. Many deities from cultures around the world are associated with fire in one or more of its forms, such as the hearth, volcanoes, and lightning.

Much later in their history, humans developed more portable forms for using sacred fires. First came the torch, then the oil lamp and candles. All holy places were lit by these miniature forms of fire, as were private home altars. Priests and magicians taught that the flame of oil lamps and candles represented the spirit's highest potential and that the smoke carried the worshipper's prayers and desires into the spiritual realm.

Herbs were either burned as incense or added to the candles. The herbs not only gave off a pleasant scent, but also often were chosen for their ability to trigger altered states that led the priest or magician into a higher state of consciousness. Accompanied by prayer, chants, dance, and/or deep concentration, the priests and magicians learned that they could manifest their desires. Thus, magic was discovered.

Magic continued to thrive and be accepted as a viable method for making life better until much later, when religions declared that magic was not possible and was only superstitious nonsense. However, these same religions continued to light their sacred places with the holy flame in one form or another.

Even today, fire rituals are still used in many cultures and religions around the world. Nearly every religion uses candles, lamps, or incense to mark their religious centers and ceremonies.

In Latin America, people still use candles to mark Halloween. They prepare an altar or a gravesite with pictures of departed loved ones and light candles that represent the spirits of the dead. In the United States and Europe, people celebrate this same seasonal festival with candles inside hollowed-out pumpkins; however, these candles are to chase away spirits, not honor them.

The Catholic religion uses an ever-burning flame, hung above the altar, to alert worshippers of the presence of the communion host. Catholic churches also have racks of votive candles, which can be lit by those presenting petitions and desires to Mary or one of the saints. Devotional candles are very popular with the worshippers of several religions. These lights may be in the form of votive, taper, or novena candles, which are offered to a particular saint, deity, or Loa (a deity in certain African religions) in a petition for their help.

To mark birthdays, several cultures use a tall candle measured into twenty-one segments. This candle is blessed and lit on the first birthday of a child. Then, it is relit on each consecutive birthday and allowed to burn down to a mark; this is repeated until the child turns twenty-one. This is enacted in the form of a petition to a deity so that the child may have a happy, healthy life. The candles commonly placed on top of a birthday cake have much the same meaning.

As far back as very ancient history, funerals have also used fire in many forms. Cremation was believed to release the soul immediately into the afterworld. Torches and candles often lined a processional path to the burial site or place of cremation, symbolically guiding the soul to the invisible door that led to Valhalla, heaven, or whatever the culture believed to be the otherworld.

Likewise, candles are often used at weddings, this time with a different connotation. The flame of the candles traditionally signals the presence of deities who will bless the union, as well as remind the bride and groom that the element of spirit should be present in the marriage.

Hanukkah is a Jewish festival known also as the Feast of Dedication or the Festival of Lights. It commemorates the victory of the Maccabees over the Syrian Greeks. The Talmud says that after the Temple was cleansed and rededicated, only one small cruse of holy oil was found to use for relighting the perpetual fire. Miraculously, this oil burned for eight days. Today, this festival is marked by lighting one candle each day, until eight candles are lit.

Another tradition found in several cultures says that when a house has known happiness and prosperity, then that dwelling is inhabited by a good spirit. When the family moves, they can carry this spirit with them by lighting a large candle from the hearth. The hearth in the new home is then lit from this candle, thus providing a welcome for the good spirit.

Several Yule or Christmas customs also use the sacred flame, although we have forgotten much of the significance behind these seasonal rituals. The lights on the modern Christmas tree have replaced the candles once used to signify rebirth. The electric light in the window was at one time a candle that helped departed loved ones return to join in the festivities. The Yule log in the fireplace symbolizes the death of the old year and the birth of the new year; it also represents the old tradition of the rebirth of the sun.

In a great many public gatherings, you will see people holding candles. Known as vigilance candles, these are used to remember a specific person or event and to create unity and change. Little do these participants realize that they are performing a type of magic. This multitude of candles actually directs the people's spiritual energy to a desired goal.

Why are candles still so popular? I believe it is because of genetic memories that lie buried deep within the superconscious mind of every human. These memories call to us over the distance of centuries; they affect our subconscious responses to life. Fire has always been sacred. Genetic memories remind us that it still is. In response, we are drawn to candles, whether we use them in ritual or simply light them on a birthday cake or the table for a special dinner.

Candle burning as a ritual attracts us. It is easy to do, primal in meaning, and a powerful form of sympathetic magic. Since magic is not a religion, a person of any religion can use it. The altar, deity-named candle or candles, and the ritual itself can be rearranged to suit your personal faith. Candle burning is comforting, as it helps us to realize we can do something about the things in our lives that we find annoying or distressing. It is spiritual in its meaning and often draws the user into a more spiritual state of mind. Powerful in its results, this form of simple magic has centuries of use behind it. It does not require fancy robes, expensive tools, or vast metaphysical knowledge to perform. It is a magical tool of the common person who desires to make her/his life better.

CHAPTER 2

The Purpose of Rituals and Magic

Because of the effectiveness of magic, and the simplicity of candle magic in particular, it has been feared by many people throughout its long history, even though candles are part of many contemporary religions.

Most candle magic is done by people who say they do not believe in magic. Candles are lit in a room simply because someone thinks it "feels" good to do it. Certain aromatic candles are used to cleanse the atmosphere and give calmness to the occupants of the house or apartment. Candlelight dinners create a romantic mood. A birthday cake with lighted candles celebrates another year of life. These are all magical, psychic, and psychological rituals that speak to the human heart. Yet they are performed by people who have no conscious intention of doing magic.

Our lives are filled with rituals, the majority of them of mundane nature. Ritual, according to *Webster's Dictionary*, is any repeated act. We routinely do certain things every day with the expectation of certain results. We brush our teeth, take a bath, eat meals, watch the news, work, and some of us may go to a religious gathering. Therefore, we are all acquainted with rituals and can understand what they are. Rituals give cohesion to our lives. It is only when ritual is connected with magic that the confusion begins.

Actually, there is nothing that mysterious about magic. Magic is simply the altering of events through will power. Ritual magic is the taking of energy from another plane of existence and weaving that energy, through certain actions, into a desired physical form on this plane of existence. A magician deliberately seeks these pools of otherworld energy, tapping into them and adding their power to the energy for manifestation that each person holds within her/himself. Because humans have a difficult time relating to abstract ideas, we call these energy pools God and/or Goddess. This otherworld energy needs two catalysts from the human magician in order to create a desire: human will power and a deep desire to accomplish a specific goal. You cannot halfheartedly do magic for something; it will not work. You must want very much the results you are striving to create; you must be totally involved in the candle ceremony—body, mind, emotions, and spirit. That is why it is easier to do magic for yourself than for others.

To do magic properly, however, may take some rethinking. The original magic of affecting an event through will power has degenerated, in most modern minds, to the acts of a stage magician, who does sleight-of-hand tricks and affects no events. There is no similarity between ritual magic and stage magic.

To prepare yourself for performing magic, you have to re-think what is possible or impossible. Magic cannot be placed under a microscope or proved in a laboratory. It lives in the mind of the user, manifesting itself in the results. When you realize that certain actions bring results, nothing is impossible.

One of the biggest hurtles to using magic is the erroneous belief that to be spiritual you cannot be concerned with material things. In defining materialism, one must understand that there is a difference between being concerned with material well-being and being controlled by material things and miser-liness. It is not wrong to use magic to have a better life. In fact, if a person's life is in a negative cycle because of lack of money or health or even love, there is no way that person can con-centrate on being spiritual. When you are content with your physical life, you are more open to expanding your spiritual life. Above all things, magic is practical.

However, it is wrong to use magic to willfully harm or con-trol others or take something that belongs to another person. Many people are surprised to learn that there are ethics in the use of magic. Magicians know that negative actions build nega-tive karma. No matter what excuse one uses for such behavior, the result is always the same: If you use negative magic, you have to pay for what you do. No bad deed goes unpunished, even if it takes some time for that punishment to fall upon the perpetrator.

This is true even of the little magic of candle burning. Think very carefully about your desire before you burn candles to get it. Never take one person away from another, or try to make someone love you or give you money. By naming a specific person in a spell, you are limiting your chances of success. Use candle magic to attract the perfect loving person for you or to bring you positive opportunities to get the money you need. You must never interfere with the free will of another person.

Neither should you do spellwork to harm physically or materially destroy someone. There are other, safer methods of bringing justice down upon evil people. For example, use your candle magic so that the law will catch and convict rapists, abusers, and murderers. Burn a candle for the swindler and con artist to be caught by his/her own actions.

This does not mean you should be a doormat about protecting yourself and your loved ones. If you are in fear of your life, do everything physically and magically within your power to eliminate the menace. Be creative in doing protective spellwork. It is essential to think through your reasons for doing magic.

Although some rituals will produce immediate results, most of them will not. It is not uncommon for a spell to take quite some time to manifest your desire. You will need to repeat the spell over a period of time, since the goal is difficult to manifest and must build up the energy it uses before manifesting. Because of this, many people who try candle-burning magic do not believe it works. They see no results in a week or a month and thus give up. Some spells need several months before their effects are seen. The time spent in empowering the more difficult spells over a period of time also gains you the biggest rewards.

Candle magic is not an instantaneous magic. It will not solve your problems overnight. However, it is a powerful tool for manifestation of your desires.

Candles and Colors

When you feel ready to try candle magic, start out with a small goal that you want to reach. By starting small, you gain confidence and experience at candle-burning magic. Use any supplies you have on hand to begin with, and get acquainted with the procedures in the rituals. However, it is not a good idea to use candles that have been burned for any other reason.

An altar is an essential piece of equipment for candle rituals. Although you can use any table or available flat surface, it is very inconvenient to have to clear away all ritual candles and tools each time you need to go about your everyday affairs. This moving of candles will also interrupt the magical energy flow. For this reason, you need to have a separate small area on which to burn your ritual candles and where you can meditate upon the purpose of your spellwork. This can be a shelf attached to the wall or a small table that will fit into one corner of a room. If possible, it is best to have this shelf or table in a room that is not readily available to visitors or anyone who might question what you are doing or who might feel free to touch or rearrange your project.

If you use a shelf, be certain that it is not under any other object, such as another shelf. The heat from the candles can scorch wood or start a fire by igniting nearby papers or books. If you use a table, position it away from draperies and other flammable materials. It is best not to have any cloths or scarves on the shelf or table. If a candle falls over, it could ignite such combustible material. Candle wax is also very difficult to get out of cloth or carpet. If you want to protect the altar top, cover it with a marble board, a metal sheet, or a thick piece of tempered glass. This protective covering also makes it easier to clean up drips of candle wax.

Eventually, you will want a few more essential items for candle-burning magic: an assortment of colors and types of candles, a number of metal holders, a candle snuffer, and perhaps a statue or two representing the deities of your spiritual path. If you use incense, you will need a holder for the sticks and cones. In a pinch, a can of sand will work for both types of incense and will provide safety from fire. You will also at some time want to include a variety of oils and small stones to enhance the power of the spells.

There are several kinds and colors of candles that are traditionally used in candle-burning magic. Lists and meanings vary from book to book. You can be as elaborate or as simple as you wish in your choices of candles and their colors. You can even burn more than one type of candle at a time if you wish. The important thing is to choose a type and color of candle that symbolizes the desire you want to manifest.

Traditionally, different kinds of candles are used for specific rituals. The most common types are the six-inch straight and the small votive candles, which can be used in place of the more elaborate types of candles. Other types of candles are explained later in this chapter.

There are always three main types of candles used in a ritual: the altar candle or candles that symbolize whatever deity you want to call upon; the astrological candle that represents you or another person; and the candle that signifies the desire you are trying to achieve. Using a nail or a small knife, inscribe identifying initials or zodiac symbols onto the astrological candles. If you do not know names, you can scratch on J for judge or OW for other woman, for example. This helps you to avoid confusion. If you do not know a person's astrological sign, choose one that most closely represents a type of person, such as Libra for a judge or Aries for someone with an aggressive attitude.

The first thing you should do after purchasing candles and taking them home is to gently clean them of any dust and debris. Do this by wiping them with a paper towel or soft cloth. If the candle is particularly dirty, you may have to wipe it with a mild soap and water solution. If it has any imperfections, carefully trim and smooth it with a knife. Then store each color of candle separately in a box or drawer. Do not put all the candles willy-nilly in the same place. It is not a good idea to store different colors directly touching each other, as the colors may bleed onto each other.

If you like to make your own candles, this will add even more energy to your spells. However, candle making is a time-consuming effort, far beyond the reaches and desires of most people. If you make your own candles, do not use the remains of old candles. The old wax still holds within it vibrations from other spells or situations. These vibrations will contaminate any spells you do with these candles.

It is also a good idea to check each candle for the power and type of vibration it holds. Purchased candles have been repeatedly handled by a number of people before they get to you. Some of these people may leave undesirable vibrations on whatever they touch. To check for this, hold a pendulum over each candle. If the pendulum swings forward and backward or in a clockwise direction, the candle's power is strong and its vibration positive. If the pendulum swings side to side or in a counterclockwise direction, the power is weak and the vibration negative. To remove negative vibrations and strengthen the power, pass the candle through frankincense incense smoke. Then test it again with the pendulum. Repeat until you get a positive answer with the pendulum.

If you plan to let candles burn out, you need to use a marble board or a thick piece of tempered glass on your altar and set each candle into a metal container or holder. This will prevent any accidents that might cause a fire. Porcelain and glass holders or containers will occasionally break from the heat.

Before you burn the small votive candles, remove the metal tab from the bottom of the candle to avoid cracking the glass container into which you put it. Better yet, coat the bottom of a small metal cauldron with an appropriate oil and set the votive candle inside to burn. Small cast-iron cauldrons are best because they take heat well. The oil will keep the wax from sticking. You should always clean away all old wax before using a holder or cauldron for another spell. If you burn seven-day candles that come in a glass container, they are ordinarily safe from breakage. If you feel uneasy about them, however, set the candle into a metal cauldron or onto a marble board.

If you burn request papers after a candle spell is finished, do not burn the paper in a cauldron or holder that still has candle wax in it. This will cause a dangerous flame that is difficult to extinguish and will be strong enough to set off smoke alarms and probably burn marks into your altar. It can also set fire to surrounding objects.

Colors are very important in candle-burning magic. However, some people have been taught to be prejudiced against certain hues. If, for example, you are not comfortable with black candles, substitute a dark blue one. Black, however, is not an evil color and definitely has its place in magic. It is the most powerful color for absorbing negative vibrations and protecting. White candles can be substituted for any color, except magenta. White, though, is not as powerful for some spells as colored candles are.

After you have worked with candle magic for a time, you will recognize certain patterns of candle-flame behavior that have traditional meanings. Even in the absence of drafts, the flames of some candles will wave and dip. This is a type of communication. If the flame bends to the north, it symbolizes that something of a physical nature is occurring. To the east, a mental aspect of the spellwork is happening. To the south, much physical energy is around the event. In the west, there are heavy emotions involved.

Some candles will also sputter and crackle, another traditional form of communication. Softly chattering candles indicate things of a personal nature are being affected. Frequent sputters mean a person of authority is influencing what happens. A candle that has strong crackles means arguments and quarrels are likely.

The strength of a candle flame also has meaning. A candle that puts out a strong, steady flame is a good sign. It indicates that a lot of power and energy are being projected into your spell. When you use figure candles, it symbolizes that one person strongly influences and possibly controls the other. A jumping flame represents raw emotions and perhaps heated arguments. A weak flame is an indication that you are facing resistance and opposition against gaining your desire. In this case, you must repeat the spell several times in order to overcome this opposition.

If a spell calls for you to burn candles for a specified length of time, then put them out and re-burn them later. Do not blow out the candles. Snuffing the flame with a candle snuffer or your fingers seals the energy into the spell instead of blowing it away.

Tradition also says you should not strike a sulfur match to light ritual candles. A lighter can be used to initially light the altar candles. Then, light a simple white candle from the altar candle and ignite the other candles with this.

If you repeat a spell using the same candles for the same purpose for several days in a row, you need to carefully trim off any drips or imperfections before beginning each ritual. This includes cleaning off any dust that might have gathered. You especially should do this with the altar or deity candles that you use for all your rituals. You want the energy of the candle spell to be as perfect as possible.

Very few spells last forever and must be worked at on a regular basis. Most spells, in fact, will need to be renewed, or repeated, if you desire the effects to be permanent and continuing. To sustain the magical effects, you should repeat the candle spells quarterly, in the proper phases of the moon. Some spells need to be repeated because they require a buildup of energy to "mature." Among these spells are those for faithfulness, marital and family happiness, healing of certain diseases, and a successful business.

You have to put feeling, effort, and time into your candle spells. Then you must have patience while you give the spell energy the time to grow and manifest what you desire.

Before you ever begin a candle spell, you need to make a list of everything you will need. This way you can be certain you have everything on hand. Then comes the most important part of any spellwork: writing down in detail exactly what you desire to manifest from the spell. Besides setting parameters for the spell, this will help you concentrate on the actual spell itself.

Setting parameters is very important in spellwork. For example, if you are working for an increase in money, you certainly do not want it to come about through an auto accident, lawsuit, an insurance claim, or a fall. You simply want the opportunity to make money honestly without harming yourself or anyone else.

When spellworking for love, always work with the goal of "a perfect love for me" in mind, never a specific person. Controlling another person and forcing him/her through magic to love you is very bad for your spiritual health, as well as your mental and emotional well-being. Not only are you limiting your happiness, which could be greater with someone else, but you are also limiting the opportunity to have the very best person for you come into your life. I have never seen a love spell directed at a specific person ever turn out happily. The forced person resents the control and will eventually break away.

The same principle applies when doing spellwork for justice or protection, although here it is safe to mention names if you are absolutely certain. You must not, however, specify punishment. When the person in question pays the price for her/his misdeeds, you do not want to be in the messy middle of it and possibly even entangled in her/his fate. Direct the spell's energy toward having the guilty party's own actions bring justice down upon her/him. Let the guilty one be caught and punished by her/his own words and deeds. In this manner, you are not involved in any way, yet have helped the scales of justice be balanced. Transfer all your hatred, sadness, and strong emotions into candle magic. In this way you can manifest your deepest desires and rid yourself of unhealthy emotional and mental turmoil, which will be changed into positive energy. After all, the best revenge is to live a good and prosperous life.

When doing candle magic, do only one spell at a time. Choose the most important need in your life and work on that first. Then, go on to another type of spell to manifest a different desire or need. You need to keep your energy centered on one thing at a time, or the spell's energy will be scrambled and the magic will dissipate before manifesting anything.

For the best results, time your rituals to the phases of the moon. For even more success, use both the correct moon phase and a particular day of the week that corresponds to your desire. The dedicated magicians often go so far as to time spells to a certain planetary hour on a certain day. Chapter 5 covers this information in more depth.

Remember, candle magic does not bring instantaneous results. It takes time for the opportunities to come that will manifest your desires.

TYPES OF CANDLES

Adam and Eve or Image candles: These candles are made in nude male and female forms, as well as a variety of colors. The figures are primarily used in spells for love and/or relationships. They are usually burned to bring love into your life. However, they can also be used to draw back a wayward lover, send away an undesirable lover, or banish an illness. Although mentioned in old Scottish records, wax images have been used as far back as ancient Egypt and Babylon.

Altar, Jumbo, or Pillar candles: These are tall, thick candles that come in various colors, usually red, white, or black. They are used as altar or deity candles since they burn too slowly to use in any other capacity. Although white is the most popular color, you may use any color that symbolizes the deities or powers with which you want to communicate. You need these candles to burn longer than the other candles, as they are lit first and extinguished last. There can be two altar candles on the altar, one on each side, or just one in the center. Some people use a seven-day candle in a glass container with a particular saint painted on the glass. Frequently, altar candles are one white and one black candle. It is not safe to leave pillar candles burning unattended, as the melted wax, which gathers in the center, can collapse one side of the candle and possibly start a fire.

Astral or Zodiac candles: These colored candles represent you and any other persons included in the spell. You may use colors from the list that follows (see pages 28–29), or choose colors that seem right to you.

Cat candles: This candle in the figure of a seated cat is used according to the color. Black will banish bad luck, break jinxes or hexes, and bring in good luck. Red helps with love. Green is used to get money or to heal, especially pets. The cat candle in black is the most popular and is often called the black cat candle.

Cross or Crucifix candles: Primarily used for protection and banishing, this type of candle can be burned as an offering to a deity, saint, or Loa. This candle will often have a rose at the crosspieces or a prayer written on it.

Devotional candles: These come in a heat-resistant glass container, usually with pictures of saints or Loas on the glass. A type of Novena candle, they are burned when asking a petition from the deities.

Double-Action or Reversing candles: Made with two colors of wax, these are used for dual purpose or reversing spells; only the lower half of a candle is dipped into another color of wax. For example, a green candle with the lower half dipped in black is for bringing in prosperity and repelling negativity and bad luck. Red dipped in black defeats the influence of anyone who is destroying your marriage or a relationship. White with black reverses all spells against you. Sometimes you can find Triple-Action candles, or candles dipped into three different colors of wax.

Memorial candles: These are usually the very largest of the votive candles that come in a glass. Ordinarily they are lit at midnight or sunrise to honor a birthday or anniversary or to remember a deceased loved one.

Mummy candles: This is a candle made in the form of a mummy figure in a coffin. It is used to ward off illness, death, or any dangerous situation. The skull candle works in much the same manner.

Satan or Devil-Be-Gone candles: This candle is made in the image of the Christian Devil. It is not for worshipping this entity, but for performing exorcisms or clearing houses of negative vibrations or spirits. It is always burned with an astral candle to represent the person or persons being harassed. The astral candle must be large enough to last longer than the Satan candle when burned.

Separation candles: This jumbo red candle is completely dipped in black wax so that all of the red color is covered. This candle should be used with extreme care and only after much honest thought, since it separates one person from the enthrallment or bondage of an undesirable person. This may be advisable when your daughter is caught in an intensive abusive relationship or marriage, or your father or mother are being conned by a swindler for all of his or her money. The break-up candle with a snake coiled around it is used for the same purposes.

Seven-Day Novena: This purchased candle has white or colored wax poured into a tall, heat-resistant glass container, often with a picture of a saint on the glass. However, you can sometimes find these without the picture. The word Novena means "new beginning" in Latin. You are to write your desire nine times on a piece of paper and tape it to the candle bottom before burning, or at least place it under the candle. Certain saints are called upon for specific help: St. Anthony for a job; San Capistrano to repel enemies; St. Jude for any court troubles; the Sacred Heart for marriage; St. Clara for any addiction problems, whether alcohol or drugs; St. Michael for total protection. Sometimes, you can also buy a seven-color, seven-day Novena candle, although these are difficult to find. With this candle, one color is burned each day for seven days.

Some Novenas are performed as nine-day rituals and use the ten- or fifteen-hour votive candles instead of one large glass-enclosed candle. The Novena is begun in the last quarter of the moon's waning phase and ends nine days later in the first quarter of the waxing moon. Nine of the votive candles are burned at a time, with replacement candles being lit from the old candle when one is close to burning out. To perform this ritual correctly, you must never let any of the candles go out before a replacement is lit.

Seven-Knob candles: Made of seven thick knobs, one on top of the other, these candles are meant to have one knob burned per day while you concentrate on your desire. The most common colors are black for banishing or releasing spells sent against you; red for setting energy into motion or removing obstacles to finding love; and green for money, manifesting, or favorable court action. Occasionally, you can find other colors of seven-knob candles: brown for delaying a court case or giving you your day in court; yellow to remove bad luck; purple for defeating psychic attack or eliminating minor health problems; blue to stop quarreling, confusion, or depression; orange for removing obstacles to a successful business or career; white to grant you a secret wish. Because it takes seven days to finish the ritual, it can be extremely powerful.

Skull candles: Made in the shape of a skull, these candles are used, not for hexing, but for healing serious, deadly, or terminal diseases. They are always burned with an astral candle.

BASIC COLORS

Black: Absorbs and removes anything; reversing, uncrossing, binding negative forces, protection, releasing, breaks up blockages, and unsticks stagnant situations. Black is also used to create confusion and discord among your enemies or repel dark magic and negative thought forms. This color is one of the most powerful available. However, be careful how you use it. If you use black for selfish, evil purposes, the energy can backlash upon you.

Blue: The uses of this color depend upon the depth of its hue. Light blue is for truth, inspiration, wisdom, protection, understanding, good health, happiness, inner peace, fidelity, patience, harmony in the home, and contacting the Higher Self. Royal blue is for happiness, loyalty, group success, occult power, and expansion. Use royal blue with caution.

Brown: This color can attract money and financial success and influence Earth elementals. It is also helpful for concentration, balance, ESP, intuition, study, to fulfill basic material needs, ground and center, and to communicate with Nature spirits. This color is powerful when used in times of financial crises.

Gold or very clear light yellow: Gold helps with great fortune, intuition, understanding, divination, fast luck (if circumstances are out of your control),and financial benefits. It attracts higher influences, money, knowledge, healing, and happiness. It is primarily associated with male deity powers.

Green: This color is associated with abundance, fertility, good fortune, generosity, material gain, wealth, success, renewal, marriage, balance, healing, and communication with Nature spirits. It can also help give a fresh outlook on life or bring balance to an unstable situation.

Indigo: This shade is a Saturn color of such a purplish-blue that it is almost black. It is useful for meditation, and it neutralizes another's magic, balances out karma, and stops another's actions. It is also used to stop gossip, lies, or undesirable competition.

Magenta: A very high vibrational frequency that tends to make things happen fast, this hue is usually burned with other candles. Burned alone, it is for quick changes, spiritual healing, and exorcism. This color is a very dark but clear red with a deep purple tint to it, a dark cranberry color. This color can be very difficult to find.

Orange: This vibrant color helps with adaptability, encouragement, stimulation, attraction, sudden changes, prosperity, creativity, enthusiasm, success, energy and stamina, and mental agility. It also discourages laziness, helps to gain control, draws good things, and changes luck. As this is a very powerful color, be certain you are willing to face major changes if you use it.

Pink: Associated with the purest form of true love, friendship, affection, romance, spiritual awakening and healing, honor, family love, and banishing hatred, this color can also banish depression and negativity.

Purple: This shade helps with success, idealism, higher psychic ability, wisdom, progress, protection, honors, spirit contact, breaking bad luck, driving away evil, divination, greater magical knowledge, spiritual protection and healing, removing jinxes and hexes, success in court cases, business success, and influencing people who have power over you. Use with caution, for purple is very powerful and the energies are difficult to handle.

Red: Associated with energy, strength, sexual potency, physical desire, passionate love, courage, will power, and good health, this color is also used to protect against psychic attack or conquer fear or laziness.

Silver or very clear light gray: Silver aids with victory, stability, helps with meditation, develops psychic abilities, removes negative powers, neutralizes any situation, and repels destructive forces. It is primarily associated with female deity powers.

White: This is used for spirituality and greater attainments in life; purity, truth, sincerity, wholeness, power of a higher nature, contacting spirit helpers, balancing the aura, confusing enemies, helping with pregnancy and birth, raising the vibrations, and destroying destructive energies. Whenever in doubt about a candle color, use white. It is a highly balanced spiritual hue.

Yellow: This brilliant color aids with intellect, imagination, power of the mind, creativity, confidence, gentle persuasion, attraction, concentration, inspiration, mental clarity, knowledge, commerce, medicine, counseling, and healing.

ASTRAL OR ZODIAC COLORS

Here, as with other candle colors, lists vary from writer to writer, so I have given choices for each sign. If the color given for your astrological sign does not appeal to you, choose a color that does.

Aries—Red, white, pink.
Taurus—Green, pink, red, yellow.
Gemini—Yellow, silver, green, red, blue.
Cancer—White, green, brown.
Leo—Gold, orange, red, green.
Virgo—Gray, yellow, gold, black.

Libra—Royal blue, light brown, black.

Scorpio—Black, red, brown.

Sagittarius—Dark blue, purple, gold, red.

Capricorn—Red, black, dark brown.

Aquarius—Light blue, dark blue, green.

Pisces—Aquamarine, royal blue, white, green.

PLANETARY COLORS

As with other color charts, planetary colors can differ greatly, depending upon the writer and the magical system they follow. Candles in these colors can be used on the appropriate days or to call upon certain energy forces. Refer to the Days of the Week section below and see chapter 5 for more information.

Earth—Browns, tans.

Jupiter—Royal blue, purples, bright blue.

Mars—All shades of red.

Mercury—Yellows, orange, yellow-green.

Moon—Silver, pink, cream, light gray, white, pale blue.

Saturn—Black, very darkest blue, very darkest purple, dark brown.

Sun—Gold, orange, deep yellow.

Venus—Pink, green, pale blue, all pastel colors.

DAYS OF THE WEEK

Candles used to symbolize a day of the week are similar to planetary candles, in that they are burned to invoke a particular planetary energy power.

Sunday—yellow, gold; the Sun.

Monday—white, silver, light gray; the Moon.

Tuesday—red; Mars.

Wednesday—purple, yellow; Mercury.

Thursday—blue; Jupiter.

Friday—green; Venus.

Saturday—black, purple; Saturn.

SEASONAL COLORS

Spring: yellow. Spring corresponds to the element of Air and the East. The time period is from the Spring Equinox in March until the Summer Solstice in June. The element of Air symbolizes mental pursuits.

Summer: red. Summer corresponds to the element of Fire and the South. The time period is from the Summer Solstice in June until the Autumn Equinox in September. The element of Fire symbolizes the physical and action. Some sources say Fire represents spirit.

Autumn: blue. Autumn corresponds to the element of Water and the West. The time period is from the Autumn Equinox in September until the Winter Solstice in December. The element of Water symbolizes the emotions.

Winter: dark green. Winter corresponds to the element of Earth and the North. The time period is from the Winter Solstice in December until the Spring Equinox in March. The element of Earth symbolizes material things.

BASIC ELEMENTAL COLORS

Most world cultures knew of and used the colors and powers of the elements. However, the placement and choice of color often differed. The ancient Mayans used: East, red; South, yellow; West, black; and North, white. Other ancient Mexican cultures had a different classification: North, red; West, yellow; South, blue; East, green; and Center, many colors together.

East: Air; yellow. Knowledge, inspiration, harmony, herbs, intellect, ideas, travel, freedom, revealing the truth, finding lost things, movement, and psychic abilities.

South: Fire; red. Change, freedom, perception, visions, spiritual illumination, learning, love, will, sexuality, energy, authority, healing, destruction, and purification.

West: Water; blue. Plants, healing, emotions, absorbing, communion with the spiritual, purification, the subconscious mind, love, friendships, marriage, fertility, happiness, sleep and dreams, and the psychic.

North: Earth; dark green. Wealth, prosperity, surrendering self-will, empathy, incorporation, business, employment, stability, success, and fertility.

Center: White. Enlightenment, finding your life path, spiritual knowledge, and seeing and understanding karmic paths in life.

TRADITIONAL ASIAN COLORS

Many Asian cultures have different magical meanings for colors. For example, they wear white for mourning the death of a loved one instead of black, as Western cultures do. With Feng Shui becoming so popular, many people will be interested in utilizing Asian colors. The five Chinese elements are very different from Western ones. Instead of Earth, Air, Fire, and Water, they are Wood, Fire, Earth, Metal, and Water. In China, one of the charts of the elements lists: North, black; West, white; South, red; East, green; and Center, yellow.

Black: Deception, dishonesty, slander, penance, and evil influences. A color of night and death, one must use great caution in combining black and red. Black is the color of the element of Water and represents Winter and the North.

Blue: Self-cultivation, consideration, and thoughtfulness.

Gold: Wealth, strength. A very fortunate color, gold is said to attract success and a good reputation. Gold is one of the colors of the element of Metal and represents Autumn and the West.

Gray: Travel and helpful people.

Green: Family, harmony, health, peace, posterity, and eternity. A restful color, green represents rebirth and new growth. Green is the color of the element of Wood and represents Spring and the East.

Pink: Marriage.

Purple or Violet: Truth and spiritual growth. Violet is a visionary color.

Red: Happiness, good fortune, a long and stable marriage, prosperity, and spiritual blessings. A revitalizing color, red is excellent for those who lack energy. Red is the color of the element of Fire and represents Summer and the South.

White: Children, helpful people, marriage, mourning, peace, purity, and travel. White is one of the colors of the element of Metal and represents Autumn and the West.

Yellow: Blessings, developing the intuition, great wisdom, and ambition. Some sources say this color is used to remember the dead and guard against evil. Yellow is the color of the element of Earth and represents the center.

TRADITIONAL NATIVE AMERICAN COLORS

The following list of color definitions is according to the Seneca tribe. Other Native American groups have their own beliefs of color meaning, which may differ.

The Navajo culture believed that different colors represented the elements: East, white; South, blue; West, yellow; and North, black. Among the Zuni it was: East, yellow; West, blue; South, red; North, white; and Center, all colors. The Cheyenne of the Plains used: East, red; South, yellow; West, white; and North, black.

Black—Hearing, harmony, listening.
Blue—Intuition, teaching, serving.
Brown—Knowing, self-discipline.
Gray—Honoring, friendship.
Green—Will, living.

Orange—Learning, kinship.
Pink—Creativity, working.
Purple—Wisdom, gratitude, healing.
Red—Faith, communication.
Rose—Seeing, motivation.
White—Magnetism, sharing.
Yellow—Love, overcoming challenges.

CHAPTER 4

The Uses of Incense, Herbs, Oils, and Stones

Although candle magic will get you results merely from burning a candle or candles, it works more efficiently if you add a few other ingredients to your spell. Oils, herbs, incenses, and small stones are easily obtained from local stores, the Internet, or mail order catalogs. If you purchase stones locally, rock shops are usually cheaper than most New Age stores.

Reliable suppliers on the Internet are www.crescentmoongoddess.com and www.Azuregreen.com.

Reliable mail order suppliers are:

Azure Green
P.O. Box 48, Middlefield, MA 01243-0048
Phone: 413-623-2155; E-mail: AbyssDist@aol.com

Pacific Spirit, The Mystic Trader
1334 Pacific Ave.,
Forest Grove, OR 97116
Phone: 800-634-9057; Fax: 503-357-1669

The reason for using the oils, herbs, and stones as part of your spellwork is not only to add the psychic energies of these materials to your work, but also to help you concentrate more deeply on the spell. As you prepare the candles, place each item on your altar in a certain position, and do each step of the candle-burning spell in a specific order. Your mind should be totally concentrated on what you are doing.

As you rub the candles from wick to end (to attract something) or from end to wick (to repel something) with an appropriate oil, concentrate on the purpose you have in mind. Roll the oiled candle in the appropriate crushed herbs, still thinking of your goal. The herbs do not have to coat the candle thickly to be effective. As you place each stone on the altar, continue to think of the purpose of your spell. See every object on the altar as another stone in the foundation of your success. The incense evokes subconscious memories that connect you with ancient magical practices.

Use an appropriate oil on each candle. This may mean that you use three or four different oils in any candle-burning ritual. It also helps to burn a compatible incense that represents the general idea of the ritual itself.

To simply set out candles without deep thought on why you are doing it takes away from the energy the spell will create. If you cannot be focused on your work, you will not obtain satisfactory results.

If the spell calls for candles to be burned only a certain length of time and then snuffed until the next night, please do not blow out the candles. Use a candle snuffer or your fingers to extinguish them. This seals the energy of the spell, instead of dissipating it.

Do *not* eat any of the herbs or drink any of the oils called for in candle magic. This can be extremely dangerous, if not deadly!

INCENSE

It really does not matter if you use incense in powered form, cones, or sticks. You are using incense to set a particular magical atmosphere. Included here is a list of appropriate scents long known for certain magical energies, scents that are often burned as part of ritual. However, you can always substitute the all-purpose scents of lotus, frankincense, or frankincense and myrrh combined in either stick or cone form.

Balance—Jasmine, orange, rose.

Banishing, release—Cedar, clove, patchouli, rose, rue, vervain.

Binding—Apple, cypress, dragon's blood, pine, wormwood.

Blessing, consecration—Carnation, cypress, frankincense, lotus, rosemary.

Changes—Dragon's blood, peppermint.

Contacting and working on the astral—Frankincense.

Creativity—Honeysuckle, lilac, lotus, rose, vervain.

Determination, courage—Allspice, dragon's blood, musk, rosemary.

Divination, clairvoyance—Acacia, cinnamon, honeysuckle, lilac, nutmeg, rose, thyme, yarrow.

Energy, power, strength—Allspice, bay, carnation, cinnamon, dragon's blood, frankincense, ginger, lotus, musk, pine, thyme, rosemary, verbena.

Exorcism—Basil, bay, cedar, frankincense, lavender, myrrh, pine, rosemary, vervain, yarrow.

Good luck, fortune, justice—Bayberry, cedar, cinnamon, honeysuckle, jasmine, lotus, mint, nutmeg, strawberry, vervain, violet.

Happiness, harmony, peace—Apple blossom, basil, cedar, clove, cypress, fir, gardenia, jasmine, juniper, lavender, lilac, lily of the valley, lotus, myrrh, orange, patchouli, rose, rosemary, vetiver, vervain, ylang-ylang.

Healing—Carnation, cedar, cinnamon, clove, cypress, eucalyptus, gardenia, lavender, lotus, myrrh, orange, peppermint, rose, rosemary, sandalwood.

Inspiration, wisdom—Acacia, clove, cypress, fir, laurel, lily of the valley, rosemary, sage.

Love—Amber, apple blossom, frangipani, gardenia, honeysuckle, jasmine, juniper, lavender, marjoram, musk, patchouli, rose, strawberry, vanilla, vetiver, violet, ylang-ylang.

Meditation—Acacia, bay, cinnamon, frankincense, jasmine, myrrh, nutmeg, wisteria.

Money, prosperity, wealth—Bayberry, bergamot, cinnamon, honeysuckle, jasmine, musk, vetiver.

Protection, defense—Basil, bay, bayberry, carnation, cinnamon, citronella, cypress, dragon's blood, fir, frankincense, jasmine, juniper, lilac, lily of the valley, lotus, marjoram, patchouli, pine, rosemary, sandalwood, vervain, violet.

Psychic abilities, opening psychic centers—Ambergris, honeysuckle, lemon, lotus, mimosa, nutmeg, wisteria.

Purification, cleansing—Basil, bay laurel, cedar, cinnamon, citronella, dragon's blood, eucalyptus, frankincense, lavender, marjoram, myrrh, peppermint, pine, rosemary, sage, thyme, vervain.

Removing hexes—Cedar, myrrh, vetiver.

Spirituality—Frankincense, lotus, myrrh, sandalwood.

Success—Ginger.

Visions—Acacia, bay laurel, frankincense, lotus.

Will power—Rosemary.

HERBS

Herbs are often used to coat oiled candles. To do this, crush the chosen herbs into small pieces and put the powdery mixture onto a paper towel. Then roll the oiled candle in this mixture. The herbs do not have to coat the candle entirely to be effective.

Herbs can also be burned on small charcoal blocks found in religious or New Age stores. The charcoal mentioned here is *not* the kind you use for a barbecue. A little goes a long way with herbs, so use a light hand when burning them. Also make certain you have adequate ventilation in any closed room in which you burn them.

Basil—A good herb for exorcising negativity from the home. Small amounts may also be sprinkled in the corners of rooms for added protection.

Bay laurel—Protection against evil; stops interference.

Catnip—Courage; love and happiness.

Chamomile—To get a marriage proposal; luck in gambling.

Clove—Banishes evil; friendship; to gain a desire.

Dandelion—Helps with clairvoyance; purifies.

Dragon's blood—Removes hexes; good luck; protection; money; love.

Frankincense—Exorcism; protection; purification; spirituality.

Ginger—Love; money; success; power.

Jasmine flower—Love; money; strengthens psychic abilities.

Juniper—A protective herb, juniper is traditionally said to protect against thieves and aid in psychic development. The mature berries can be strung on a thread and hung in the house to attract love.

Lavender—Love; money; attracts helpful spirits.

Lemon verbena—Drives away evil; helps to repel someone who loves you, but whom you do not love.

Lily of the valley—Poisonous, so do not eat or leave where children or pets can find it! Known to attract peace and knowledge, it is easier to use the oil than the plant.

Marigold—Also called calendula and pot marigold. Flowers added to pillows give clairvoyant dreams.

Marjoram—Also called sweet marjoram and pot marjoram. Soak marjoram, mint, and rosemary in pure water. Use this water to sprinkle throughout the house for protection.

Mugwort—Protection; strengthens psychic abilities, especially in divination.

Myrrh—Purification; protection; spirituality.

Nutmeg—Aids in gambling and lotteries; luck; love; prosperity; fertility.

Orris root—Attracts the opposite sex; aids in divination.

Patchouli—Breaks up any spell; money; brings back a lost love; helpful in defeating enemies.

Peppermint—Purification; love; increases psychic ability.

Pine—A purification incense to be burned can be made by mixing equal parts of dried juniper, pine needles, and cedar.

Rose petals—Love; happiness in the home.

Rosemary—Healing for headaches; exorcism; keeps a lover faithful.

Rue—The ancient Celts used this herb as a defense against spells and dark magic. When burned in purification or exorcism incenses, it repels negativity and gets things moving. Also attracts the right love for you.

Sage—Purification; protection; wisdom.

Saint John's Wort—Happiness; healing; courage; love; protection; helps with divination.

Sandalwood, red—Exorcism; healing; protection; spirituality; gaining your wish.

Sandalwood, yellow—Protection; exorcism; spirituality.

Thyme—Also called common thyme and Mother of thyme. Make a tea of thyme and marjoram to add to a bath, thus cleansing your aura. It is also used in pillows to cure nightmares.

Vervain—Also called holy herb and verbena. When burned, this herb repels psychic attack. However, it is also useful for purification, gaining love, and attracting wealth.

Wormwood—Removes hexes; repels black magic; aids with the psychic.

Yarrow—Primarily used for divination and love spells, this herb is said to have the power to keep couples happily married.

OILS

Candles are frequently rubbed with scented oil from wick to end (to attract something) or from end to wick (to repel something). As you do this, concentrate on the purpose you have in mind. Candles can be used with only the oil or oil and herbs. If called for, roll the oiled candle in the appropriate crushed herbs, still thinking of your goal.

Amber—Happiness; love.

Bayberry—Prosperity; protection; gaining control of a situation.

Bergamot—Money; happiness; optimism.

Carnation—Healing; strength; protection.

Cedar—Purification; healing; removes hexes.

Cinnamon—Money; purification; energy.

Clove—Healing; stimulates creativity.

Dragon's blood—Protection; purification; removes hexes; exorcism.

Frangipani—Love; attracts the perfect mate.

Frankincense—Protection; purification; spirituality.

Frankincense and myrrh—Purification; protection; healing; great spirituality.

Gardenia—Peace; love; healing; harmony; happiness.

Heliotrope—Attracts wealth; protection.

High John the Conqueror—Aids in all endeavors; strengthens the mental abilities; protection; removes hexes.

Honeysuckle—Money; strengthens psychic abilities.

Jasmine—Love; money; brings psychic dreams.

Juniper—Protection.

Lavender—Healing; love.

Lilac—Protection; wards off evil.

Lotus—Protection; purification; spirituality.

Magnolia—Balance with Nature; oneness.

Musk—Attracts the opposite sex; sexual love; prosperity.

Myrrh—Breaks hexes; protection; spirituality; healing; aids in psychic development.

Patchouli—Love; protection; purification.

Peppermint—Energy; stimulates creativity; money.

Pine—Strength; protection; purification.

Rose—Love; cleanses the atmosphere of a room or home; fertility.

Rosemary—Energy; protection.

Sage—Purification; finding wisdom and the truth.

Sandalwood—Spirituality; cleansing.

Vanilla—Sexual love; aids in mental powers.

Vetiver—Removes hexes; money; love.

Violet—Gain luck; love; protection; aids in finding wisdom for a solution.

Yarrow—Courage; exorcism; strengthens the psychic.

Ylang-Ylang—Love; harmony.

Planetary Oils

Planetary oils are used when you desire to strengthen certain planetary energies in your life or in more advanced magical spells.

Jupiter—Anise, lime, magnolia, nutmeg, sage, sandalwood.

Mars—Allspice, carnation, dragon's blood, ginger, honeysuckle, peppermint, pine.

Mercury—Bayberry, lavender, lemon grass, lily of the valley, peppermint.

Moon—Coconut, eucalyptus, gardenia, jasmine, lotus, myrrh, sandalwood, water lily, white rose, wintergreen.
Saturn—Black orchid, hyacinth, patchouli, water violet.
Sun—Cedar, clove, cinnamon, frankincense, juniper, rosemary, rue.

STONES

When using stones to amplify your candle magic, there are two ways to choose them. You may use the general description by color to choose the stones you need, or you may use the more specific list by magical description.

Stones do not need to be faceted, fancy, or expensive to work. Stones found in a natural state or tumbled until smooth can be just as effective as expensive ones.

There are certain stones that can be used with any candle burning. Clear quartz crystal is so powerful and all embracing that you can substitute it for other stones or add it to groupings of other stones to amplify their energy. Fluorite also amplifies the energies of other stones, regardless of its color. Carnelian will speed up the manifestation of your desire. Lodestone will help in any ritual where you are attempting to attract something into your life. The little-used spectrolite can manifest results in any situation that may require a "miracle" to see results.

It is important to wash your stones carefully before use. A few stones in the following lists should not be washed with water or put into salt for cleansing. Calcite is an example of a stone that should not be washed, and turquoise should not be placed in salt. Also, hold them in the smoke of frankincense or frankincense and myrrh incense to give them positive vibrations.

Stones by Color

Black—Binding; defense by repelling dark magic; transforming negative spells and thoughtforms into positive power; general defense; release from feeling bound.

Blue—Harmony; understanding; journeys or moves; healing.

Brown—Contacting Earth elementals; success; amplifies all Earth magic and psychic abilities; common sense.

Green—Marriage; relationships; balance; practical creativity, particularly with the hands; fertility; growth; money.

Indigo—Discovering past lives; understanding karmic problems; balancing out karma; stopping undesirable habits or experiences.

Orange—Change your luck; power; control of a situation.

Pink—Healing; true love; friendship.

Purple—Breaking bad luck; protection; psychic and spiritual growth; success in long-range plans.

Red—Courage to face a conflict or test; energy; taking action.

White—Spiritual guidance; being directed into the right paths; calmness; becoming centered; seeing past all illusions.

Yellow—Power of the mind; creativity of a mental nature; sudden changes.

Clear quartz crystal—Psychic work; helps with divination; amplifies the power raised during all spellwork.

Lodestone or magnet—Drawing power; ability to attract what you desire.

Moonstone—Gaining occult power; soothing the emotions; rising above problems; Moon deities.

Pyrite or fool's gold—Money, prosperity, total success; Sun deities.

Stones by Magical Powers

Abuse, surviving—Iolite, jasper, kunzite, lapis lazuli, obsidian, smoky quartz, rhodocrosite, spinel, tourmaline, .

Accidents, preventing—Carnelian, chalcedony, malachite, spinel, topaz, turquoise.

Anger—Chrysocolla, jade, marble, peridot, rhodonite, ruby, serpentine, topaz.

Artists—Aventurine, emerald, quartz crystal, tourmaline.

Astral travel—Moss agate, carnelian, galena, lodestone, meteorite, petrified wood, quartz crystal, sapphire, shell, zircon.

Attracting the perfect mate—Aventurine, lapis lazuli, malachite, rose quartz, ruby.

Authorities or government, influencing—Bloodstone.

Bad habits—Agate, amazonite, citrine, obsidian.

Balance—Agate, amethyst, aquamarine, aventurine, calcite, carnelian, chrysoprase, emerald, ivory, jade, kunzite, lepidolite, lodestone, malachite, moldavite, moonstone,

obsidian, onyx, opal, quartz crystal, rhodocrosite,
serpentine, sodalite, spectrolite, sugilite, tanzanite,
thulite, tiger's eye, topaz, tourmaline, turquoise,
vanadinite, obsidian.

Beauty—Alabaster, chalcedony.

Binding troublesome people—Agate, beryl, bloodstone, chrysoprase, coral, emerald, hematite, jet, malachite, black
obsidian, black onyx, pyrite.

Blockages, removing—Aventurine, calcite, jasper, kunzite,
malachite, quartz crystal, rhodocrosite, ruby, sapphire,
shell, sodalite, obsidian.

Burglars, deterring—Topaz.

Business—Amethyst, citrine, garnet, jade, malachite,
marble, obsidian, opal, quartz crystal, sard, serpentine,
spinel, tourmaline.

Calming—Adularia, agate, amber, amethyst, aquamarine,
aventurine, chrysoprase, coral, fossils, ivory, jade,
kunzite, lapis lazuli, lepidolite, marble, onyx, peridot,
quartz crystal, rhodocrosite, rhodonite, serpentine,
sodalite, tanzanite, topaz, tourmaline, zircon.

Change of luck—Aquamarine, aventurine, azurite, bloodstone, chalcedony, citrine, fluorite, garnet, hawk's eye,
hematite, iolite, lapis lazuli, malachite, moonstone,
peridot, petrified wood, pyrite, rhodonite, sardonyx,
staurolite, tiger's eye.

Changing vibrations—Agate, quartz crystal.

Changes—Amethyst, obsidian, peridot, quartz crystal, smoky quartz.

Children—Coral, lapis lazuli, quartz crystal.

Cleansing—Azurite, lapis lazuli, opal, peridot, quartz crystal, selenite.

Communications—Agate, amazonite, aventurine, beryl, chrysocolla, garnet, lapis lazuli, malachite, moldavite, sodalite, spinel, tourmaline, turquoise.

Concentration—Carnelian, fluorite, quartz crystal, spinel, topaz, tourmaline.

Conflicts—Agate, tourmaline.

Consciousness-altering—Quartz crystal.

Control—Garnet, hawk's eye, jet, onyx, sapphire, thulite.

Courage—Agate, diamond, hematite, jade, ruby, serpentine.

Court cases, lawyers, influencing the law—Amethyst, aquamarine, chalcedony, hematite, jade, lodestone, sard, serpentine.

Creativity—Agate, amazonite, amethyst, apatite, aquamarine, aventurine, chrysocolla, chrysoprase, emerald, jade, lapis lazuli, malachite, obsidian, onyx, opal, quartz crystal, sapphire, serpentine, sodalite, spinel, topaz, tourmaline, turquoise.

Cycles in life—Obsidian, tiger's eye.

Dark magic, defeating—Amethyst, holey stones, mica, obsidian, onyx, peridot, petrified wood, pyrite, quartz crystal, sapphire, sard, topaz, tourmaline.

Deceptions, uncovering—Moonstone.

Deflecting negativity—Beryl, jasper, quartz crystal.

Demonic possession, removing—Jet, black obsidian.

Depression, relieving—Garnet, jade, jet, lapis lazuli, serpentine, topaz.

Destiny—Peridot, quartz crystal.

Discrimination—Agate, spinel.

Divination, scrying—Agate, amethyst, hawk's eye, beryl, cat's eye, crocidolite, emerald, fluorite, mica, moonstone, obsidian, quartz crystal, rhodocrosite, tiger's eye, tourmaline. (See Psychic abilities.)

Dreams, prophetic—Agate, amethyst, emerald, jade, quartz crystal, rhodocrosite, serpentine.

End of the rope, totally discouraged—Malachite.

Enemies, defeating—Aquamarine.

Energy, gaining—Agate, andalusite, beryl, goldstone, jasper, quartz crystal, rhodocrosite, rhodonite.

Energy shield—Tektite or meteorite, rhodocrosite, tourmaline.

Evil spirits, repelling—Agate, bloodstone, carnelian, crocidolite, jade, jasper, malachite, obsidian, onyx, serpentine, tourmaline.

Excessive energy, removing—Fluorite.

Family problems—Carnelian, sard.

Fear—Amber, aquamarine, aventurine, chrysocolla, citrine, coral, fossils, obsidian, tourmaline.

Feminine energies—Chrysocolla, jade, moonstone, turquoise.

Fertility—See Pregnancy and Creativity.

Fire, protecting against—Topaz.

Friends—Agate, geode, iolite, lapis lazuli, ruby, sard, topaz, tourmaline, turquoise, zircon.

Gaining spiritual blessings—Amethyst, apatite, citrine, diamond, emerald, lapis lazuli, moldavite, opal, pearl, petrified wood, sapphire, sugilite, black tourmaline.

Gambling luck—Aventurine, lodestone.

Giving thanks—Citrine, lapis lazuli, pearl, quartz crystal, sapphire, sugilite.

Goals, making—Adularia, amethyst, azurite, calcite, chrysoprase, citrine, diamond, hawk's eye, hematite, iolite, snowflake obsidian, peridot, rhodocrosite, sodalite, topaz, watermelon tourmaline.

God—Amethyst, ammonite, quartz crystal.

Goddess—Amethyst, ammonite, jet, moonstone, quartz crystal, shell.

Good luck—Agate, amethyst, aventurine, carnelian, holey stones, lodestone, onyx, opal, petrified wood, sapphire, sard, staurolite, tiger's eye, topaz.

Grief—Obsidian, tourmaline.

Grounding—Agate, fluorite, obsidian, smoky quartz, serpentine, tiger's eye, zircon.

Guardian angels—Quartz crystal.

Guilt, releasing—Chrysocolla, tourmaline.

Hallucinations, controlling—Jasper.

Happiness—Moss agate, amazonite, amethyst, garnet, marble, ruby, sapphire, sard, zircon.

Harmonizing—Aventurine, calcite, coral, jade, lapis lazuli, lepidolite, obsidian, quartz crystal, serpentine, sodalite.

Healing—Moss agate, amazonite, amber, amethyst, aquamarine, beryl, bloodstone, boji stones, carnelian, chrysocolla, citrine, emerald, flint, fluorite, garnet, hematite, jade, jasper, lapis lazuli, malachite, pearl, rhodocrosite, ruby, sapphire, tourmaline, turquoise.

Higher teachings—Azurite, fluorite, jade, quartz crystal, ruby, sapphire, spectrolite, ugilite, tourmaline.

Hope—Amazonite.

House, home—Garnet, jade, marble, sard, serpentine.

Illusions, seeing through—Amethyst, azurite, chalcedony, pyrite, sodalite.

Ill-wishing, repelling—Carnelian, coral, sard.

Improbable situations, handling—Spectrolite.

Information, gaining—Azurite, quartz crystal, sapphire.

Inner guidance—Bloodstone, quartz crystal.

Insomnia, treating—Agate.

Inspiration—Amazonite, amethyst, aquamarine, azurite, garnet, onyx, peridot, pyrite, quartz crystal, sapphire, tourmaline.

Inspiring creativity—Amazonite, amethyst, apatite, chrysocolla, citrine, tsavorite garnet.

Intellect—Agate, amber, jade, lapis lazuli, rhodocrosite, serpentine, topaz, tourmaline.

Intolerance, removing—Beryl, morganite.

Intuition—Amethyst, aquamarine, azurite, citrine, malachite, opal, peridot, quartz crystal, ruby, sapphire, sodalite, topaz, tourmaline.

Jealousy, dissolving—Peridot.

Job, career—Carnelian, lapis lazuli, obsidian, scapolite.

Justice—Amethyst, jade, serpentine.

Karma—Calcite, citrine, jade, jet, obsidian, onyx, quartz crystal, serpentine, shell, tiger's eye, topaz.

Lawsuits—See Court cases, lawyers, influencing the law.

Laziness, curing—Beryl.

Leadership—Iolite, opal, ruby, spinel.

Long life—Moss agate, beryl, onyx.

Love—Aquamarine, aventurine, calcite, coral, emerald, lodestone, malachite, moonstone, rose quartz, ruby, zircon.

Marriage—Aquamarine, sard.

Meditation—Amethyst, azurite, calcite, coral, emerald, fluorite, geode, jade, malachite, moldavite, obsidian, quartz crystal, serpentine, shell, sugilite, tanzanite, turquoise.

Memory—Amethyst, beryl, carnelian, coral, emerald, opal, rhodocrosite, topaz.

Money—Agate, amber, bloodstone, calcite, lodestone, malachite, obsidian, opal, spinel, tourmaline, zircon.

Moves—Bronzite, jade, serpentine.

Natural disasters, surviving—Spinel.

Negative vibrations, shielding against—Hematite, jade, serpentine.

New beginnings—Agate, emerald, opal, tourmaline.

Nightmares, troubled sleep, removing—Chalcedony, garnet, holey stones, jasper, topaz.

Obstacles, overcoming—Agate, hematite.

Opportunity—Garnet.

Past lives—Amethyst, coral, fluorite, fossils, garnet, geode, hematite, jasper, malachite, moonstone, obsidian, opal, petrified wood, quartz crystal, rhodocrosite, shell, staurolite, tiger's eye, tourmaline.

Patience—Danburite, spectrolite.

Personal power—Agate, cinnabar, jasper, obsidian, opal, plasma, quartz crystal, ruby.

Poverty, reversing—Sapphire.

Pregnancy—Dioptase, lapis lazuli, rose quartz.

Privacy—Jasper, sapphire.

Prophecy—Amethyst, bloodstone, moonstone, obsidian, opal, quartz crystal, tiger's eye, topaz, tourmaline.

Prosperity—Agate, amber, aquamarine, aventurine, blood-stone, cat's eye, chalcedony, citrine, crocidolite, emerald, garnet, jade, malachite, marble, opal, pyrite, sapphire, yellow topaz, green tourmaline, turquoise, green zircon.

Protection—Eye agate, amethyst, aquamarine, aventurine, beryl, bloodstone, calcite, carnelian, cat's eye, chalcedony, chrysoprase, emerald, epidote, flint, garnet, hematite, holey stones, iolite, jasper, jet, lapis lazuli, malachite, moonstone, black obsidian, obsidian, black onyx, pearl, petrified wood, pumice, pyrite, ruby, sapphire, sard, sunstone, tiger's eye, black tourmaline, turquoise, zircon.

Psychic abilities, gaining—Agate, amethyst, apatite, azurite, beryl, crocidolite, heliodor, jet, moonstone, opal, quartz crystal, sapphire, sodalite, spinel, sugilite, tanzanite, tiger's eye, tourmaline, turquoise.

Psychic abilities, strengthening—Adularia, moss agate, Apache tear, apatite, aquamarine, beryl, fluorite, jet, moonstone, peridot, blue topaz, purple tourmaline.

Psychic attack, stopping—Obsidian, smoky quartz, turquoise.

Public speaking—Carnelian, emerald. (See Communications.)

Purification—Aquamarine, quartz crystal, tourmaline.

Regeneration—Alexandrite, garnet, quartz crystal, tourmaline.

Relationships—Chrysocolla, pyrite, sapphire.

Releasing—Apatite, aventurine, chalcedony, chrysocolla, chrysoprase, jade, moonstone, morganite, petrified wood, quartz crystal, sodalite, tourmaline.

Responsibility—Aquamarine.

Secret enemies, revealing—Moonstone.

Security—Agate, petrified wood.

Self-confidence—Amazonite, aventurine, bloodstone, carnelian, chalcedony, citrine, garnet, iolite, ivory, quartz crystal, rhodonite, sard, spinel, tourmaline.

Self-love—Calcite, ivory, quartz crystal.

Sexual attractiveness—Obsidian, opal, sodalite, sunstone.

Solving problems—Jade, quartz crystal, serpentine.

Soul friends—Amethyst, quartz crystal.

Soul mates—Quartz crystal.

Speech—See Public speaking.

Speed up manifestation—Carnelian, quartz crystal.

Spirit guides, teachers—Moss agate, citrine, diopside, lapis lazuli, moonstone, obsidian, opal, pearl, quartz crystal, spinel, sugilite, topaz, tourmaline, zircon.

Spiritual awareness—Amethyst, apatite, calcite, emerald, hiddenite, labradorite, lepidolite, moonstone, onyx, pearl, quartz crystal, rhodonite, sphalerite, sugilite, tiger's eye, vanadinite.

Spiritual growth—Amber, amethyst, citrine, diamond, emerald, lapis lazuli, ruby, sapphire.

Spiritual mates—Quartz crystal.

Stamina—Jade, labradorite.

Stubbornness—Agate, beryl, goshenite, tiger's eye.

Studying—Carnelian, quartz crystal, topaz, tourmaline.

Success—Andalusite, obsidian, sard.

Survival—Chrysocolla, flint, fossils, jade. (See Abuse, surviving.)

Telepathy—Quartz crystal, spinel.

Tension and stress, removing—Agate, amethyst, hematite, jade, lapis lazuli, moonstone, obsidian, peridot, pyrite, quartz crystal, rhodonite, serpentine, zircon.

Third eye—Moss agate, amethyst, azurite, quartz crystal, sodalite, tiger's eye.

Time travel—Galena, fossils, geode, lodestone, quartz crystal.

Trance—Quartz crystal, sapphire, spinel.

Transformation—Alexandrite, amethyst, ametrine, azurite, fluorite, garnet, jasper, malachite, onyx, quartz crystal, ruby, shell, tourmaline.

Travel—Coral, quartz crystal.

Truth—Agate, calcite, chrysoprase, emerald, galena, geode, pearl, pyrite, quartz crystal, sapphire, tiger's eye, topaz.

Unwanted situations, handling—Iolite, malachite.

Useless sacrifices, stopping—Quartz crystal.

Victory—Agate, chrysoprase, diamond, jet.

Visionary—Adularia, agate, amethyst, holey stones, malachite, quartz crystal.

Visualization—Aventurine, quartz crystal.

Vitality—Moss agate.

Will power—Hematite, pyrite.

Writers—Amethyst, aventurine, garnet, sapphire, spinel, tourmaline.

CHAPTER 5

Timing by the Moon and Days

To ensure the greatest probability of success for your candle rituals, you should time them to correspond with certain phases of the moon and do them on specific days of the week. To help you determine the correct dates for all the moon's phases, buy a good astrological calendar that gives accurate moon measurements.

The full moon is when the moon is completely lit, big and round. When the moon is growing in size, it is referred to as the waxing moon. The waxing moon cycle runs from the day after the new moon until the day of the full moon. The day and night of the full moon is the strongest part of this cycle. This is the time to do spellwork for beginning new projects, prosperity, growth, love, success, harmony, peace, and all positive energy projects. Basically, the waxing moon is for increase, growth, building, and gain.

The new moon is when no light is seen from the moon at all; it is completely dark. When the moon is decreasing in size, it is referred to as the waning moon. The waning moon cycle runs from the day after the full moon until the day of the next new moon. The day and night of the new moon is the strongest of this cycle. This is the time for dissolving any negatives, protection, neutralizing hostile situations, removing bad habits, and terminating unhealthy relationships or situations. The waning moon is for decrease, destruction, banishing, binding, and removal.

Each day of the week is traditionally connected with a specific planet, deity, and function. Monday is the Moon; Tuesday, Mars; Wednesday, Mercury; Thursday, Jupiter; Friday, Venus; Saturday, Saturn; and Sunday, the Sun. By carefully studying the religious pantheon of your choice, you can correspond any deities to the days of the week, instead of using the listed deity interpretations.

Using moon phases and planetary days and hours in magical rituals goes back to ancient Babylon and perhaps beyond. Many ancient cultures knew of the seven closest planetary bodies and considered them important and powerful enough to influence the lives of humans. These planets were also said to correspond to the days of the week and the hours of each day. Although moon phases are crucial to the power raised in a candle spell, using the correct day and hour will further enhance the buildup of energy to manifest your desire. However, you do not have to use days and hours if you do not wish to do so.

The idea behind using planetary days and hours is that you are connecting with a stronger energy for use in candle rituals. To use this system, decide which planet best symbolizes the type of ritual you plan to do. Then, from the charts in this chapter, select the proper day and hour in which to do the ritual. When reading the hour charts, always make adjustments for Daylight-Saving Time.

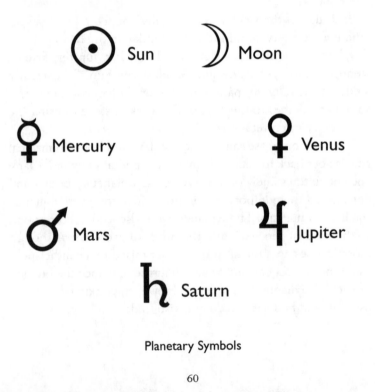

Planetary Symbols

A.M.	Mon	Tues	Wed	Thurs	Fri	Sat	Sun
1:00	☽	♂	☿	♃	♀	♄	☉
2:00	♄	☉	☽	♂	☿	♃	♀
3:00	♃	♀	♄	☉	☽	♂	☿
4:00	♂	☿	♃	♀	♄	☉	☽
5:00	☉	☽	♂	☿	♃	♀	♄
6:00	♀	♄	☉	☽	♂	☿	♃
7:00	☿	♃	♀	♄	☉	☽	♂
8:00	☽	♂	☿	♃	♀	♄	☉
9:00	♄	☉	☽	♂	☿	♃	♀
10:00	♃	♀	♄	☉	☽	♂	☿
11:00	♂	☿	♃	♀	♄	☉	☽
12:00	☉	☽	♂	☿	♃	♀	♄

A.M. Hours

P.M.	Mon	Tues	Wed	Thurs	Fri	Sat	Sun
1:00	♀	♄	☉	☾	♂	☿	♃
2:00	☿	♃	♀	♄	☉	☾	♂
3:00	☾	♂	☿	♃	♀	♄	☉
4:00	♄	☉	☾	♂	☿	♃	♀
5:00	♃	♀	♄	☉	☾	♂	☿
6:00	♂	☿	♃	♀	♄	☉	☾
7:00	☉	☾	♂	☿	♃	♀	♄
8:00	♀	♄	☉	☾	♂	☿	♃
9:00	☿	♃	♀	♄	☉	☾	♂
10:00	☾	♂	☿	♃	♀	♄	☉
11:00	♄	☉	☾	♂	☿	♃	♀
12:00	♃	♀	♄	☉	☾	♂	☿

P.M. Hours

PLANETARY COLORS AND POWERS

Jupiter: Colors are royal blue and purples. Stones are lapis lazuli, amethyst, turquoise, and sapphire. Incenses are lilac, nutmeg, and cedar. Use on Thursday for good luck, winning over great odds, honor, more of what you have in abundance, social pleasures, family reunions, male fertility, to get a raise or promotion, health, friendships, the heart's desires, trade and employment, group enterprises, legal matters, harmony, accomplishment, and expansion of things in your life.

Mars: Colors are all shades of red. Stones are bloodstone, garnet, red agate, ruby, and red topaz. Incense is dragon's blood. Use on Tuesday for power over enemies, overcoming obstacles, courage, conflict, surgery, physical strength, opposition, defense, endurance, victory, politics, difficulties in lawsuits, to seek paroles, peaceful separations, gambling, athletics, to change the weather, to divert storms, destruction, and protection.

Mercury: Colors are orange, pale yellow, violet, and multicolored. Stones are carnelian, fire opal, and agate. Incense is white sandalwood. Use on Wednesday for creativity, mental sharpness, memory, business, medicine, diplomacy, counseling, changes, divination, eloquence, speed, speech, writing, poetry, and healing of nervous disorders.

Moon: Colors are silver, lavender, cream, light gray, pearl-white, and pale blue. Stones are moonstone, clear quartz crystal, beryl, and pearl. Incenses are white rose, myrtle, mugwort, camphor, lily, jasmine, and lotus. Use on Monday for travel, visions, divinations, dreams, magic, love, agriculture, domestic life, medicine, luck, feminine aspects, calming and controlling emotions, journeys for pleasure, plant growth, female fertility, birth, and healing women's problems. Avoid performing spells during a lunar eclipse.

Saturn: Colors are black, very darkest blue, very darkest purple, and dark brown. Stones are onyx, jet, pearl, and star sapphire. Incenses are poppy, myrrh, civet, and storax. Use on Saturday for knowledge, familiars, death, reincarnation, protection, binding, overcoming curses, retribution, duties, responsibilities, finding lost objects, to reveal secrets, recovering stolen goods, to collect a debt, to influence others, intuition, overcoming blocks and removing obstacles.

Sun: Colors are gold and deep yellow. Stones are zircon, jacinth, goldstone, yellow topaz, and yellow diamond. Incenses are heliotrope, orange blossom, cloves, frankincense, ambergris, musk, cinnamon, and vanilla. Use on Sunday for health, healing, confidence, hope, prosperity, leadership, happiness, personal fulfillment, life-energy, promotion, swift success, new money, instant action, theatrical success, release from captivity, support of those in power, political influence, friendships, active change, and creativity. Avoid performing spells during a solar eclipse.

Venus: Colors are green, pale blue, and pink. Stones are amber, malachite, jade, peridot, coral, emerald, and turquoise. Incenses are apple blossom, musk, verbena, rose, and red sandalwood. Use on Friday for love, marriage, harmony, music, pregnancy, friendship, pleasure, artistic creativity, fertility, partnerships, sex, spiritual harmony, children, the emotions, and instincts.

CHAPTER 6

Candle Spells

Before you begin a candle spell, be certain you have all the needed materials on hand. Choose the spell you wish to use, and make a list of all candles and their colors, any oils, herbs, stones, and anything else that will be needed. If you cannot find seven-knob or seven-day candles, use seven of the straight or votive candles instead.

If a candle spell is for more than one burning or to be continued for a certain number of days, try to repeat the spell at the same time each day. When you are finished with any candle burning, carefully gather up the remaining wax and paper ashes and safely dispose of them.

When anointing candles, always use only a small amount of oil. Then, wipe your hands carefully before proceeding with the ritual. To use oil in a seven-day, glass-enclosed candle, simply put a few drops on the top of the candle and carefully spread it around.

Herbs can be used with candle burning in three simple ways. After oiling a candle, you can roll it lightly in crushed herbs (discussed in chapter 4), or you may sprinkle the herbs in a circle around the lit candles. If you use incense to be burned on charcoal, you may sprinkle the herbs on the coals. Only a small amount of herbs is required for any of these procedures. If you do not care for the incense, herbs, and oils listed, you can always substitute other appropriate ones from chapter 4. Frankincense, combined frankincense and myrrh, and lotus are good all-purpose incenses.

Many of the herbs can be found right in your kitchen. Herbs such as basil, allspice, nutmeg, ginger, cloves, cinnamon, and sage are commonly used in cooking. Finding lemon verbena need not be a problem if you have a small area for growing this herb. The dried leaves can also be used in a delicious tea without harmful effects. However, although it is easily cultivated by even the blackest of gardening thumbs, lemon verbena tends to spread and will take over existing flowerbeds unless you vigorously keep it within bounds.

Check for the correct phase of the moon and the proper day for candle magic. If the phase of the moon is not a good one for the type of ritual you will be doing, reschedule the spellwork for a more appropriate time. If you have an emergency and need to take action immediately, by all means do the ritual whatever the moon phase. There will be some benefit, although it will be less powerful. When the moon next enters the more auspicious phase, repeat the ritual for better results.

Although some candle spells specifically call for a seven-day ritual, all candle burning with straight or votive candles always has a more powerful effect if repeated three, five, seven, or nine times.

Write out your desire so you can see if you have it clearly in mind. You want to create opportunities to gain what you desire, instead of depend on random chance to fulfill it. For example, you do not want your spell for money to be fulfilled through an injury or death. In this case, state that you wish a positive opportunity to gain money to come your way.

Remember the law of karma. If you deliberately harm someone or break up a relationship so you can have one of the partners, you will eventually pay a heavy price for such unethical behavior. Besides doing the spell for the wrong reasons, such as greed, jealousy, or revenge, you are also limiting yourself and interfering with the free will of another. Think how you would respond if someone tried to manipulate and control you through magic.

SETTING UP A GENERAL ALTAR

It is best to set up your general altar and meditate there before you ever begin to do candle magic. This helps to build up an atmosphere of power around your altar, an atmosphere that will enhance your spellwork and make it more effective.

Supplies: Choose a table, chest, or shelf that is not in the central living area and is in a place where it will not be disturbed. Also check for anything nearby that might be a fire hazard.

You will need either a white pillar or seven-day candle to set in the central back portion of your altar, or one white pillar candle and one black one, one to set on each end of the altar toward the back. Traditionally, the black candle sits on the left side of the altar, the white on the right. If you use the two altar candles, you can place an image, picture, or symbol of a deity between them, in the central rear portion of the space.

Have a lighter and a plain white candle available at all times for lighting the other candles; never light the other candles with the lighter. You will also find it convenient to keep nearby a nail or other sharp instrument for carving names onto candles, a supply of small squares of papers, and a metal cauldron or bowl for burning them. Put the incense holder on the left side of the altar. If you want to burn a candle to symbolize the powers of a particular day, place it in a holder on the right side. This leaves the center of the altar open for your candle-burning spells.

Use metal or nonflammable holders for all your candles, especially the ones you leave to burn out completely.

If you want to place a picture of a person or pet (such as for healing) on the altar during your rituals, you can easily make what is called a placket to enclose it. A placket is two square or rectangular pieces of cloth or felt, sewn together on three sides only. This leaves a kind of pocket. You can slip a photo, letter, or paper inside on which a person's name is written, and keep it safe from candle wax, oil, dust, and prying eyes. You can make plackets in several colors if you wish, although white is considered to be an all-purpose color. You will find it convenient to have several plackets on hand for your work.

Advice: If possible, you should leave this basic altar set up at all times. By meditating near it, you build a store of energy there before you begin to do candle spells. Always light your altar candles first, then the incense, then the day candle. Extinguish the candles in the reverse order. The incense is left to burn out.

Whenever a chant is given in a candle spell, you can substitute an appropriate psalm or other text according to your belief system.

Unless stated differently in a spell, use the six-inch straight or small votive candles.

See Fig. 1, on page 147.

ABUNDANCE

Change Your Luck

Candles—Straight or votive candles in the following colors: your astrological color, one orange (sudden change), one silver or light gray (neutralization of bad luck), one black (remove bad luck), and one magenta (to hurry the luck-changing process).

Oil—Lotus.

Herbs—Basil.

Incense—Lotus or frankincense.

Stones—Four pieces of carnelian or four clear quartz crystals.

Other Supplies—None.

Timing—The full moon.

Day—Thursday.

Advice—Changing your luck is sometimes the only way to obtain prosperity, health, love, or a new job. You need to rid yourself and your life of negative vibrations before positive vibrations can enter.

Spellwork—Light the altar candles and the incense. Anoint the black candle from the end to the wick; the others from the wick to the end. Place the black candle in the center of your working space. Set your astrological candle in front of the black, with the other candles joining it in a circle around the central black candle. Place a stone beside each of these four candles.

Light the astrological candle and say: "This is me and everything that represents me." Light the black candle and say: "This is my bad luck. It now leaves me. I shed no tears over the parting." Light the silver candle and say: "This neutralizes any remnants of bad luck. They dissolve into nothingness." Light the orange candle: "This represents the changes for good that are coming into my life. I welcome them with open arms." Light the magenta candle: "This is the astrological energy that I need to speed up the change."

Sit for at least five minutes, repeating to yourself: "I welcome change. I welcome the incoming good." Do not allow any thoughts of failure or bad situations to enter your mind during this time.

Leave the candles to burn out completely. Dispose of the wax afterward.

See Fig. 2, on page 147.

Attract Money

Candles—Straight or votive candles: your astrological candle; one green (material gain), one brown (attract money), and one gold (financial benefits).

Oil—Bergamot or cinnamon.

Herbs—Nutmeg.

Incense—Cinnamon or honeysuckle.

Stones—Agate and garnet.

Other Supplies—Small nail.

Timing—The full moon or the waxing moon cycle.

Day—Sunday.

Advice—The Attract Money spell is not for long-term prosperity or for an unlimited supply of money. It is for a specific amount of quick money to pay off the bills piling up on the table.

Spellwork—Light the altar candles and the incense. Using the nail, inscribe the brown candle with three dollar signs representing money: $$$. Below this, carve in the amount you need. Anoint the candles from the wick to the end. Set the brown candle in the center of your altar working space with your astrological candle behind it. Set the gold candle on the left of the brown candle and the green candle on the right. Place the agate between the gold and brown, and the garnet between the brown and green. Light the candles from left to right. Say the chant five times. Leave the candles to burn out completely. Dispose of the wax afterward.

Chant—One, two, three, four,
Money knocking on my door.
Five, six, seven, eight,
A jingling purse is my fate.

See Fig. 3, on page 148.

Gain Prosperity

Candles—A green (material gain) seven-day, glass-enclosed candle or a double-action green candle. Four orange (attraction, sudden changes, success) straight or votive candles.

Oil—Bayberry or bergamot.

Herbs—Vervain.

Incense—Bayberry or jasmine.

Stones—Bloodstone and malachite.

Other Supplies—Small nail.

Timing—On the full moon or the waxing moon cycle.

Day—Thursday.

Advice—Prosperity gained through the use of magic will continue only as long as you use it responsibly. It also needs to be renewed at regular intervals.

Spellwork—Light the altar candles and the incense. Using a nail, carve a dollar sign into the green portion of the double-action candle or into the top of the glass-enclosed candle. Inscribe a lightning bolt into each of the orange candles. Anoint the double-action candle and the orange candles from the wick to the end, or just the top of the enclosed candle. Set it in the center of your workspace. Arrange the orange candles around the central green candle. Place the malachite on one side of the central candle, the bloodstone on the other. Light the central green candle, then the orange ones. Say the chant. Leave the candles to burn out completely. Dispose of the wax afterward. If you wish, you may burn four new orange candles each day until the seven-day green candle is gone.

Chant—Worries gone, finances clear,
Security comes for one full year.
I wrap myself in prosperity.
As I will, so shall it be.

See Fig. 4, on page 148.

Influence Someone to Repay a Debt

Candles—A green (material gain) seven-knob candle or seven green straights or votives and four yellow (gentle persuasion) straight or votive candles.

Oil—Jasmine.

Herbs—Clove.

Incense—Ginger, jasmine, or allspice.

Stones—Hematite and tiger's eye.

Other Supplies—None.

Timing—On the full moon or the waxing moon cycle.

Day—Saturday.

Advice—Be certain the debt is actually owed to you before doing this spell. If you think someone owes you a debt, but it is not true, you will find yourself being forced to pay back any debts *you* owe. This spell also works for people who borrow things and don't bother to return them.

Spellwork—Light the altar candles and the incense. Inscribe the name of the person who owes you the debt on the seven-knob green candle. Anoint the candles from the wick to the end. Set the green candle in the center of your working space. Set the yellow candles around the green one, with the stones inside this circle. Light the green candle first, then the others. Say the chant seven times. Leave the yellow candles to burn out completely. Dispose of the wax afterward. Burn only one knob of the green candle each night. If you wish, you may burn new yellow candles each night until the seven-knob candle is gone.

Chant—What was given in trust shall be freely returned.

        What was mine shall be mine again.

See Fig. 5, on page 149.

CAREER OR JOB

Increase Personal Power

Candles—Straight or votive candles in the following colors: one silver (victory, stability), one yellow (confidence, concentration), and one purple (success, wisdom).

Oil—Carnation.

Herbs—Red sandalwood or rue.

Incense—Carnation, frankincense, or pine.

Stones—Agate, jasper, and black obsidian.

Other Supplies—None.

Timing—On the full moon or the waxing moon cycle.

Day—Thursday.

Advice—Increasing your personal power is a positive action only when you are trying to build up your self-esteem or want to stand up to someone who is manipulating or bullying you. It is not a positive action if you use this spell to gain power so that you can control others.

Spellwork—Light the altar candles and the incense. Anoint the candles from the wick to the end. The candles are set out in a triangular pattern with the silver at the top, the yellow at the bottom right, and the purple at the bottom left. Place the black obsidian near the silver candle, the jasper near the yellow, and the agate near the purple. Light the candles in the same order, beginning with the silver. Say the chant. Leave the candles to burn out completely. Dispose of the wax afterward.

Chant—Power of the self, I seek.

　　　　Strength to be bold, not weak.

　　　　Courage to stand straight and tall,

　　　　Power to overcome all.

See Fig. 6, on page 149.

Conquer Fear

Candles—Straight or votive candles in the following colors: one silver (stability), one light blue (inspiration, inner peace, contacting the Higher Self), one pink (banish depression), and one red (strength, courage).

Oil—Musk.

Herbs—Sage.

Incense—Allspice, dragon's blood, or musk.

Stones—Amber and black obsidian.

Other Supplies—None.

Timing—On the full moon or the waxing moon cycle.

Day—Saturday.

Advice—This spell is particularly useful when you fear public speaking, facing someone who has intimidated you in the past, flying on a plane, or tackling a new project. Although you are working to eliminate fear, you are doing this by drawing in the necessary cosmic energy to help you conquer this fear.

Spellwork—Light the altar candles and the incense. Anoint the candles from the wick to the end. Set the silver candle near the center of your working space with the light blue in front.

Place the red on the right side, the pink on the left. Put the black obsidian in front of the silver candle and the amber in front of the light blue one. Light them in any order. Meditate for several minutes on absorbing the energy coming from the candles. Visualize yourself facing your fear and being triumphant. Say the chant. Leave the candles to burn out completely. Dispose of the wax afterward.

Chant—All fear is washed away,

Only courage with me will stay.

I am in control of my destiny.

As I will, so shall it be.

See Fig. 7, on page 150.

Find a New Job

Candles—Straight or votive candles in the following colors: one black (break up blockages, remove negatives), one gold (fast luck, happiness), and one green (success, material gain).

Oil—Pine or peppermint.

Herbs—Dragon's blood or ginger.

Incense—Jasmine, peppermint, or pine.

Stones—Carnelian and lapis lazuli.

Other Supplies—None.

Timing—On the full moon or waxing moon cycle.

Day—Thursday.

Advice—No magical spell will work unless you do your part to help. This means you must actively seek a new job, not sit back and wait for it to fall into your lap.

Spellwork—Light the altar candles and the incense. Anoint the black candle from the end to the wick; the others from the wick to the end. Place the black candle on the left, the green in the center, and the gold on the right. Put the carnelian between the black and green candles, and the lapis lazuli between the green and gold candles. Light the candles in the same order as you set them out. Say the chant. Sit for several moments, thinking of the type of job you want. Leave the candles to burn out completely. Dispose of the wax afterward.

Chant—Doors to new opportunities open before me.

No obstacles stand in my way.

Only the best of employment comes to me.

Good luck draws a new day.

See Fig. 8, on page 150.

Attain Success

Candles—Orange seven-knob candle. Seven straight or votive candles in each of the following colors: light blue (inspiration, patience, inner peace) and magenta (fast action, success). If you cannot find an orange seven-knob candle, substitute seven orange straights or votives, one to be burned each day.

Oil—Peppermint.

Herbs—Ginger or vervain.

Incense—Ginger or rosemary.

Stones—Sard and black obsidian.

Other Supplies—None.

Timing—On the full moon or the waxing moon cycle.

Day—Thursday.

Advice—The definition of success varies from person to person. Decide what success means to you personally before you do this spell.

Spellwork—Light the altar candles and the incense. Anoint the candles from the wick to the end. Set the orange seven-knob candle in the center of your workspace. Inscribe "harmony" on the light blue candle and "success" on the magenta candle. Place the light blue candle on the left of the seven-knob candle and the magenta on the right, with the piece of sard in front of the blue candle and the black obsidian in front of the magenta. Light the seven-knob candle first, then the others. After one knob has burned, extinguish all the candles. Repeat the spell the next day when you again relight the candles. Say the chant. Allow the seven-knob candle to burn down one knob, while leaving the other candles to burn out completely. Dispose of the wax afterward.

Chant—Success is beautiful. I attract success.

Opportunities are bountiful. I attract opportunities.

A new cycle of life begins. I accept the new cycle.

See Fig. 9, on page 151.

Inspire Creativity

Candles—Straight or votive candles in the following colors: one orange (creativity, enthusiasm) and one yellow (creativity, imagination, inspiration).

Oil—Lilac or rose.

Herbs—Rose petals.

Incense—Lilac, lotus, or rose.

Stones—Amethyst, chrysocolla, black onyx, and turquoise.

Other Supplies—None.

Timing—On the full moon or the waxing moon cycle.

Day—Wednesday.

Advice—Creativity is more than writing, painting, or music. It can be coming up with a new idea for a birthday party, some innovative business method, or how to redecorate your home. Pregnancy can also count as creativity, so this spell can be used to get pregnant.

Spellwork—Light the altar candles and the incense. Anoint the candles from the wick to the end. Place the orange and yellow candles side by side in the center of your workspace. Put the black onyx behind the orange candle and the turquoise in front of it. With the yellow candle, place the chrysoprase behind and the amethyst in front of it. Light the candles. Say the chant. Meditate on the particular reason you need creativity. Leave the candles to burn out completely. Dispose of the wax afterward.

Chant—The universe is filled with endless ideas of creativity.
I attract them to me like a magnet.
My mind and dreams are open to these ideas.
They flow in like a stream of clear water.

See Fig. 10, on page 151.

GENERAL LIFE PATH

Overcome a Bad Habit

Candles—Straight or votive candles in the following colors: one black (remove anything negative), one light blue (good health, happiness, inner peace), and one orange (sudden changes, success).

Oil—Cedar or peppermint.

Herbs—Basil or bay laurel.

Incense—Dragon's blood, peppermint, or cedar.

Stones—Jade, rhodonite, or topaz.

Other Supplies—Small nail; small piece of paper.

Timing—On the new moon or the waning moon cycle.

Day—Tuesday.

Advice—This is one spell you cannot do for another person. No habit can be broken unless there is a sincere desire to quit.

Spellwork—Light the altar candles and the incense. Inscribe the name of the habit on the black candle. Anoint it from the end to the wick and set it in the center of your workspace. Write "peace" on the light blue candle and "success" on the orange candle. Place the orange candle to the left of the black candle and the light blue on the right. Put the jade in front of the orange candle, rhodonite in front of the black, and topaz in front of the light blue. Light the black candle first, then the others. Say the chant nine times. Leave the candles to burn out completely. Dispose of the wax afterward.

Chant—I walk away from harmful things.
           I walk into the Light.
           I draw my strength from endless Love,
           And from this win my fight.
See Fig. 11, on page 152.

Stop Arguments

Candles—Straight or votive candles in the following colors: one black (remove negatives), one indigo (balance out karma, stop lies), and one silver (neutralize the situation, repel destructive forces).

Oil—Patchouli.

Herbs—Patchouli.

Incense—Allspice, cedar, or patchouli.

Stones—Bloodstone, black obsidian, and black onyx.

Other Supplies—Small nail.

Timing—On the new moon or the waning moon cycle.

Day—Tuesday.

Advice—This spell should not be used to gain the upper hand over someone, but rather to sincerely bring peace and harmony.

Spellwork—Light the altar candles and the incense. With the nail, inscribe the names of the quarreling parties on the black candle and set it in the center of your workspace. Be sure to include your own name if you are involved. Anoint the black candle from the end to the wick; the others from the wick to the end. Place the indigo candle on the left and the silver one on the right. Place the stones in front of the candles: black obsidian in front of the black, black onyx in front of the indigo, and the bloodstone in front of the silver one. Light the black candle first, then the others. Say the chant. Sit for several minutes, visualizing the quarreling parties completely bathed in white light. Leave the candles to burn out completely. Dispose of the wax afterward.

Chant—Peace, harmony, friendship, and joy.

Only these shall surround you.

Only these shall remain with you.

Peace, harmony, friendship, and joy.

See Fig. 12, on page 152.

Settle Disturbed Conditions in a Home

Candles—Seven straight or votive candles in the following colors: light blue (harmony in the home), silver (neutralize a negative situation), and yellow (gentle persuasion, healing). One candle of each color is burned each night for seven nights. A seven-knob candle in each color may be substituted, with one knob burned each night.

Oil—Patchouli.

Herbs—Frankincense or myrrh.

Incense—Frankincense or patchouli.

Stones—Hematite and agate.

Other Supplies—None.

Timing—On the full moon or the waxing moon cycle.

Day—Tuesday.

Advice—Disturbed conditions, such as constant dissension and general unhappiness, can vary in intensity, depending upon the seriousness of the events occurring. These conditions make those who live in the home uncomfortable and irritable.

Spellwork—Light the altar candles and the incense. Anoint the candles from the wick to the end. Set the candles in a straight line with the light blue on the left, silver in the middle, and yellow on the right. Place the hematite between the blue and silver, and the agate between the silver and yellow. Light the candles from left to right. Say the chant. Leave the candles to burn out completely. Dispose of the wax afterward.

Chant—Your (My) home is filled with peace and love.

No negatives shall enter there (here).

Harmony shall reign with peace and love.

This I decree for one full year.

See Fig. 13, on page 153.

Learn the Truth About a Situation or Person

Candles—Seven straight or votive candles in the following colors: white (truth, purity) and light blue (truth, wisdom). One candle of each color is to be burned each night for seven nights.

Oil—Carnation.

Herbs—Sage or yellow sandalwood.

Incense—Clove, cypress, or sage.

Stones—Chrysoprase, a geode, and tiger's eye.

Other Supplies—None.

Timing—On the full moon or the waxing moon cycle.

Day—Monday.

Advice—This spell is not to be used for snooping or to satisfy curiosity. It is of value when you need to know the hidden truth of a person for business reasons or if you are romantically involved.

Spellwork—Light the altar candles and the incense. Anoint the candles from the wick to the end. Set the white and blue candles side by side in the center of your working space. Place the chrysoprase behind the white candle and the tiger's eye behind the blue one. Set the geode between the two candles. Light the candles. Say the chant. Leave the candles to burn out completely. Dispose of the wax afterward.

Chant—Whatever the truth may be,

Reveal it to me.

Give me the knowledge to use truth wisely.

Grant me clear sight.

See Fig. 14, on page 153.

Release Situations or People from Your Life

Candles—Straight or votive candles in the following colors: one black (remove negative forces), one light blue (happiness, wisdom, inner peace), and one brown (ground and center).

Oil—Lilac or patchouli.

Herbs—Lemon verbena.

Incense—Patchouli or cedar.

Stones—Aventurine, jade, petrified wood, and clear quartz crystal.

Other Supplies—Small metal cauldron; small piece of paper.

Timing—On the new moon or the waning moon cycle.

Day—Saturday.

Advice—Think carefully before deciding to remove situations or people from your life. If they are creating adverse or negative effects, then they deserve to be removed, but not if it is merely a retaliatory whim of the moment. Remember, to help the spell, you must also do your part to take action.

Spellwork—Light the altar candles and the incense. Anoint the black candle from the end to the wick; the others from the wick to the end. The candles are arranged in a triangular shape with the cauldron in the center. Set the black candle at the back of the cauldron, the light blue in front and to the left and the brown in the front and to the right. Set the stones around the cauldron. Write on the paper the situations or people you want to move out of your life. Light the candles in the same order as you set them out. Say the chant. Light the paper from the black candle and drop it into the cauldron to burn. Allow the candles to burn completely out. Dispose of the wax and ashes.

Chant—I cut all ties that bind me.

> All negatives that block my way
> Shall disappear as morning dew
> In the light of a brand new day.

See Fig. 15, on page 154.

Accept a Situation

Candles—Straight or votive candles in the following colors: one yellow (mental clarity, confidence), one silver (neutralize a situation), and one white (purity, truth, sincerity).

Oil—Gardenia.

Herbs—Frankincense.

Incense—Rose, orange, or musk.

Stones—Sard and amazonite.

Other Supplies—None.

Timing—On the full moon or the waxing moon cycle.

Day—Tuesday.

Advice—This spell is to be used when you know you should not walk away from a situation, but see it through. This is not for control of the situation, but to help you cultivate an attitude of acceptance and non-hostility until either the problem is resolved or you can walk away from it.

Spellwork—Light the altar candles and the incense. Anoint the candles from the wick to the end. Place the candles in a straight line from left to right: white, silver, and finally the yellow. Put the sard between the white and silver candles, and the amazonite between the silver and yellow ones. Light the candles from left to right. Say the chant. Leave the candles to burn out completely. Dispose of the wax afterward.

Chant—I accept my karma to be in this time and place.
Give me the strength and courage to endure
what I must.

Grant me the peace and wisdom I need to endure.
See Fig. 16, on page 154.

Find Happiness

Candles—Straight or votive candles in the following colors: one pink (friendship, spiritual healing), one light blue (inner peace, harmony, patience), and one gold (healing, happiness).

Oil—Lily of the valley.

Herbs—St. John's Wort.

Incense—Jasmine or rose.

Stones—Moss agate and amethyst.

Other Supplies—Small nail; a flower you like.

Timing—On the full moon or the waxing moon cycle.

Day—Friday.

Advice—All happiness must come from within yourself. It is not someone else's responsibility to make you happy. This spell helps you to see the truth within yourself and to come to terms with that.

Spellwork—Light the altar candles and the incense. Using a nail, inscribe the word "love" on the pink candle, "peace" on the light blue one, and "success" on the gold candle. Anoint the candles from the wick to the end. Place the flower in the center of your working space; it should be a flower that in some manner represents happiness to you. Set the candles in a triangular shape with the gold one at the top, the pink at the bottom left, and the light blue at the bottom right. Place the agate between the gold and pink candles, and the amethyst between the gold and blue ones. Light the gold candle first, then the others. Say the chant three times. Leave the candles to burn out completely. Dispose of the wax afterward.

Chant—Open my life to happiness and joy.

Fill my life with the wonder of peace and love.

Open my eyes to the incoming happiness.

Make me aware of all the good that comes into my life.

See Fig. 17, on page 155.

Consecrate a Talisman

Candles—Straight or votive candles in the following colors: one red (will power, strength), one silver (stability), and one black (binding all negative forces).

Oil—Frankincense or lotus.

Herbs—Frankincense or yellow sandalwood.

Incense—Lotus or frankincense.

Stones—Bloodstone, black onyx, and black obsidian.

Other Supplies—The jewelry or item you plan to use as a talisman.

Timing—On the full moon or the waxing moon cycle.

Day—Monday.

Advice—A talisman acts like a good luck charm. It is something you wear or carry with you to help you cope with life and the unexpected.

Spellwork—Light the altar candles and the incense. Anoint the black candle from the end to the wick; the others from the wick to the end. Place the red candle with the bloodstone above it at the top point of a triangular pattern. Set the silver candle and the black obsidian in front of it and to the left, and the black candle with the black onyx in front of it and right. Hold the talisman in the incense smoke for several minutes. Then place it in the center of the triangle. Light the red candle, then the black, followed by the silver. Say the chant. Leave the talisman in place until the candles have burned completely out. Leave the candles to burn out completely. Dispose of the wax afterward. Wear or carry the talisman until the next full moon, when it should be reconsecrated.

Chant—I bind you with protection and light,

      So that protection and light is all that you return

        to me.

      This is my will. So shall it be.

See Fig. 18, on page 155.

Reach a Decision

Candles—Straight or votive candles in the following colors: one yellow (intellect, confidence), one orange (success, energy), and one gold (intuition, fast luck).

Oil—Lotus.

Herbs—Rue.

Incense—Sage, acacia, or lotus.

Stones—Agate and clear quartz crystal.

Other Supplies—Small metal cauldron; small piece of paper.

Timing—On the full moon or the waxing moon cycle.

Day—Tuesday.

Advice—Before doing this ritual, take time to think out all the possibilities of your decision carefully. Afterward, you must do everything you can to take action. This spell will bring you wisdom to help make the correct decision, not have it made for you.

Spellwork—Light the altar candles and the incense. Anoint the candles from the wick to the end. Although the candle pattern will be a triangular shape, the point of the triangle will point to the right where the cauldron sits. Set the gold candle behind the yellow one. Then place the orange candle to the center right of these candles. Put the cauldron to the right of the orange candle. Situate the clear quartz crystal above the cauldron and the point toward it, the agate below the cauldron. Write out exactly what decision you need to make and place the paper inside the cauldron. Light the gold candle, then the yellow, and finally the orange candle. Say the chant three times slowly. Light the paper from the orange candle and drop it into the cauldron to burn. Leave the candles to burn out completely. Dispose of the wax and ashes afterward.

Chant—Grant me the wisdom to make a choice.

> Give me the spiritual guidance to do what is right.
> Fill me with courage to take the right stand.
> Grant me the wisdom to make my decision.

See Fig. 19, on page 156.

Start a New Venture

Candles—Straight or votive candles in the following colors: one purple (success in business, wisdom), one gold (good fortune, fast luck, money), and one brown (financial success, balance).

Oil—Cinnamon.

Herbs—Nutmeg.

Incense—Cinnamon, rosemary, or clove.

Stones—Agate and emerald.

Other Supplies—None.

Timing—On the full moon or the waxing moon cycle.

Day—Thursday.

Advice—Do not perform this candle ritual until you have settled on only one new venture. If you do this spell while thinking of several possibilities, you will get a muddled, unclear answer or result.

Spellwork—Light the altar candles and the incense. Anoint the candles from the wick to the end. Set the candles in a straight line, purple on the left, gold in the middle, and brown on the right. Put the agate between the purple and gold candles, and the emerald between the gold and brown ones. Light them from left to right. Say the chant. Meditate on the new venture you want to undertake. Leave the candles to burn out completely. Dispose of the wax afterward. This ritual and meditation may be repeated each night, if you wish, until the next new moon.

Chant—A new road opens before me.

A new cycle begins its round.

I step out in courage and wisdom.

To me success is bound.

See Fig. 20, on page 156.

Peaceful Divorce

Candles—A seven-day candle in light blue (inner peace, harmony), plus seven straight candles each of black (protection, binds negative forces) and indigo (balance out karma). You can use seven light blue straight candles instead of the seven-day candle, and burn one each day with the other colors.

Oil—Patchouli.

Herbs—Lemon verbena.

Incense—Patchouli or vervain.

Stones—Sodalite and chalcedony.

Other Supplies—Seven new straight pins; placket with photo of divorcing couple.

Timing—On the new moon or the waning moon cycle.

Day—Tuesday.

Advice—It is extremely unusual for a divorce to end amicably. Somewhere during the process, animosities inevitably seem to arise. Try to be as fair as possible, leaving aside thoughts of revenge, even though you may feel you have just cause. You should aim instead for a fair, swift, and peaceful separation. Only then can your life come back into balance and open up new opportunities for you.

Spellwork—Light the altar candles and the incense. Anoint the top of the seven-day candle and put it in the center of your altar workspace. Anoint the black candle from the end to the wick; the others from the wick to the end. Place the placket containing a photo, if possible, or at least a paper with both names on it before the seven-day candle. Lay the chalcedony and sodalite on top of the placket. Make a circle of the black candles around the placket and seven-day candle. Carefully push a straight pin in each indigo candle about halfway down. Then arrange the indigo candles around the black candles in another circle on the outside of the black ones. Light the seven-day candle first, then the black candles, and finally the indigo ones. Say the chant. Leave the seven-day candle burning at all times, but extinguish the other candles after an hour. Relight them each day at the same time and again say the chant.

Chant—These pins I do not wish to burn.

'Tis (name)'s mind I wish to turn.

May she/he not know peace or rest

Until she/he grants my request.

See Fig. 21, on page 157.

Celebrate a Birth

Candles—Straight or votive candles in the following colors: one pink (love, spiritual awakening, family love), one green (fresh outlook on life), and one gold (happiness, good fortune).

Oil—Rose.

Herbs—Rose petals.

Incense—Frankincense or myrrh.

Stones—Lapis lazuli and rose quartz.

Other Supplies—Placket with a photo or name of the new baby.

Timing—Preferably, on the full moon or the waxing moon cycle.

Day—Monday.

Advice—This ritual can be performed at any time within a month after the birth. If you adopt a child, you can use this same ritual when you receive the child. Receiving an adopted child counts as a birth, for it truly is just that.

Spellwork—Light the altar candles and the incense. Anoint the candles from the wick to the end. Put a placket containing a photo of the child or the name on a piece of paper before the deity image on your altar. Place the lapis lazuli and rose quartz on top of the placket. Arrange the candles in a straight line, pink on the left, green in the middle, and gold on the right. Light the candles from left to right. Say the chant. Leave the candles to burn out completely. Dispose of the wax afterward.

Chant—We light these candles in joy for the new life in
our midst.
May love and goodness always surround her
(him, or child's name).
May Light always guide her (him, or child's name).
May good health and prosperity always fill her
(his, or child's name) life.

> May happiness and contentment always be on
> her (his, or child's name) doorstep.
> We welcome you, child of Light and love.

See Fig. 22, on page 157.

Celebrate a Wedding Anniversary

Candles—Straight or votive candles in the following colors: one gold (good fortune, understanding), one red (physical desire, good health), and one white (sincerity, wholeness).

Oil—Rose.

Herbs—Rose petals.

Incense—Frankincense or myrrh.

Stones—Aquamarine and sard.

Other Supplies—A photo of the couple, or some symbol important to them.

Timing—On the full moon or the waxing moon cycle.

Day—Friday.

Advice—This candle ceremony can be performed as a private affair for the couple or can be done during a gathering of sympathetic and understanding friends and family. Every anniversary of a relationship that survives the constant ups and downs of life is reason for celebration.

Spellwork—Light the altar candles and the incense. Put a symbol of the marriage in front of the deity image on your altar. This symbol can be a photo of the couple, a spiritual wedding gift that has special meaning to them, saved flowers or cake from the wedding itself, or simply a nice card with their names carefully done in calligraphy. Place the aquamarine to the left of this symbol and the sard to the right. Anoint the candles from the wick to the end. Arrange the candles in a straight line before this, gold on the left, red in the center, and white on the right. Light the candles from left to right. Say the chant. Leave the candles to burn out completely. Dispose of the wax afterward.

Chant—True love found us and brought us together.

True love bound our hearts together as one.

May true love always fill our hearts and our days

As we continue our journey through life.

See Fig. 23, on page 158.

In Memory of a Deceased Loved One

Candles—Straight or votive candles in the following colors: one purple (spirit contact, spiritual healing) and one white (purity, truth, wholeness).

Oil—Patchouli.

Herbs—Patchouli.

Incense—Patchouli or lotus.

Stones—Four pieces of clear quartz crystal.

Other Supplies—Photo of the deceased person.

Timing—This spell can be used on the loved one's birthday, the day of their death, or on a full moon or during a waxing moon cycle.

Day—Saturday.

Advice—It takes a very long time for the heart and mind to heal after losing someone. The pain never completely goes away, but it does become more bearable with time. A remembrance, such as this candle ritual, is a good healing method. Holding back the sorrow and tears is never healthful. Allow anyone present to cry and express him or herself. Just keep a full box of tissue on hand. Such remembrances often bring remaining family and friends closer together.

Spellwork—Light the altar candles and the incense. Place a photo of the deceased person before the deity image on your altar. Put one clear quartz crystal to the left and right of the photo. Anoint the candles from the wick to the end. Set the purple candle on the left of the photo, and the white candle on the right. Light the candles. Say the chant. Leave the candles to burn out completely. Dispose of the wax afterward.

Chant—Gone from this Earth, but not forgotten.

Gone from our sight, but not from our hearts.

Memories comfort our sorrow.

We know we shall meet again.

See Fig. 24, on page 158.

Giving Thanks

Candles—Straight or votive candles in the following colors: two white (truth, sincerity), one light blue (inner peace, harmony, contacting the Higher Self), and one pink (affection, healing).

Oil—Lotus or frankincense.

Herbs—Sage.

Incense—Frankincense or myrrh.

Stones—Amethyst, clear quartz crystal, and iolite.

Other Supplies—Small metal cauldron; small piece of paper.

Timing—On the full moon or the waxing moon cycle.

Day—Sunday.

Advice—Giving thanks for little things, as well as big ones, helps one to grow spiritually and have a better insight into life in general. This ritual can be worked once a month or whenever an important event occurs. It is especially nice to do after having a successful candle ritual manifestation.

Spellwork—Light the altar candles and the incense. Write on the paper exactly what you are thankful for. Set the cauldron with the paper inside it in the center of your working space. Place the amethyst, clear quartz crystal, and iolite around the cauldron. Anoint the candles from the wick to the end. The white candles go behind and in front of the cauldron, while the blue candle is set on the left side and the pink on the right. Light the candles. Say the chant. Leave the candles to burn out completely. Dispose of the wax and ashes afterward.

Chant—I give thanks to the Goddess (God)

>   For the blessings showered upon me.

>   I ask for continued blessings.

>   So it is. So shall it be.

See Fig. 25, on page 159.

HEALING

General Healing 1

Candles—A red or blue figure candle to represent the sick person. Red figure candles are easier to find than blue ones. Nine candles each of the following colors: gold, green, pink, purple, red, silver, yellow, and white.

Oil—Carnation, myrrh, or lavender.

Herbs—Frankincense.

Incense—Lotus or lavender.

Stones—Amber and turquoise.

Other Supplies—Small nail; placket with photo or name.

Timing—Waxing moon cycle.

Day—Sunday (health, healing), Thursday (good health), Monday (emotional medicine), or Wednesday (physical medicine).

Advice—Always make certain the person for whom the healing is done actually wants to be healed. Some people subconsciously do not want a healing. Their illness gives them leverage to control those around them. With such a person, no amount of healing will take effect.

Spellwork—Light the altar candles and the incense. Using a nail, carve the sick person's name or initials into the figure candle. Anoint the candles from the wick to the end. Arrange the turquoise and amber on each side of the figure candle. A placket containing a photo of the sick person, or a paper with their name, is placed in front of the figure candle. The other candles are arranged in two interlocking squares around the figure candle.

On the inside square, the gold candle is set behind the figure, the green to the right, the pink in front of it, and the purple to the left. On the outer square, the red goes between the gold and purple, silver between gold and green, yellow between green and pink, and white between pink and purple.

To begin the spell, anoint the figure candle with lavender, carnation, or myrrh oil from the wick to the bottom. Lay it on its back on a paper towel in the center of your altar. Light the surrounding candles, beginning with those in the inner square. Say the chant. Pray or meditate, visualizing great rays of white light streaming down upon this candle. Leave the other candles to burn out.

On the second day, stand the figure candle on its feet, facing the altar. Again anoint it with healing oil, say the chant, and visualize the white light. Light the surrounding candles and meditate. Leave the other candles to burn out.

On the third day, anoint the figure candle again and stand it facing the altar. This time, light the candle and the surrounding candles. Say the chant. Pray or meditate again, visualizing the sickness leaving the person's body and being burned to nothing in the brilliant white light. This time leave all the candles to burn out. Dispose of the wax.

You can repeat this spell twice more for a count of nine days. If you do this, always start each spell-cycle of three days with a fresh figure candle.

Chant—Healing comes from the Light.

You are filled with Light.

Healing comes from Universal Love.

You are filled with Universal Love.

All shadow of disease disappears under the Light.

You are healed and whole again.

See Fig. 26, on page 159.

General Healing 2

Candles—Straight or votive candles of the colors of: one gold (healing, happiness), one green (renewal, balance), one pink (spiritual awakening, healing), one purple (drive away evil, healing), one red (energy, courage, good health), one silver (neutralize a situation, remove negatives), one yellow (confidence, healing), and one white (wholeness, balance the aura).

Oil—Clove or gardenia.

Herbs—Myrrh.

Incense—Jasmine or myrrh.

Stones—Beryl and fluorite.

Other Supplies—Placket with photo of the sick person.

Timing—On the full moon or the waxing moon cycle.

Day—Sunday (health, healing), Thursday (good health), Monday (medicine), or Wednesday (medicine).

Advice—Always make certain the person for whom the healing is done actually wants to be healed. Some people subconsciously do not want a healing. Their illness gives them leverage to control those around them. With such a person, no amount of healing will take effect.

Spellwork—Light the altar candles and the incense. Place the placket containing the sick person's photo or a paper with their name in the center of your working space. Set the beryl to the left side of the placket and the fluorite to the right. Anoint the candles from the wick to the end. The candles go in a doubled square around this. On the upper left corner of the square, arrange the gold and white candles, the upper right the pink and green. On the lower right, set the red and purple candles, and on the lower left, set the yellow and silver ones. Light the candles, beginning with the upper left ones and working clockwise around the square. Say the chant. Leave the candles to burn out completely. Dispose of the wax afterward.

Chant—I call in the Light of healing,
>   To fill the body, mind, and spirit of (name).
>   The Light cannot be denied its healing powers.
>   No one and nothing can stop it from its
>   cleansing path.
>   I draw down the Light! I draw down the Light!

See Fig. 27, on page 160.

General Healing 3

Candles—Straight or votive candles in the following colors: one gold (healing happiness), one green (renewal, balance, healing), one pink (spiritual healing, banish depression), one purple (spiritual protection and healing), one red (energy, will power, good health), one silver (remove negative powers), one yellow (power of the mind), and one white (purity, wholeness).

Oil—Gardenia.

Herbs—Rue.

Incense—Sandalwood or gardenia.

Stones—Lapis lazuli and tourmaline.

Other Supplies—Small metal cauldron; paper with the sick person's name.

Timing—On the full moon or the waxing moon cycle.

Day—Sunday (health, healing), Thursday (good health), Monday (medicine), or Wednesday (medicine).

Advice—Concerning a person to be healed, read the advice in General Healing 1. (See page 101.)

Spellwork—Light the altar candles and the incense. Write the sick person's name on the paper. Place the cauldron in the center of your working space, with the paper inside it. Set the lapis lazuli on the left of the cauldron and the tourmaline on the right. Anoint the candles from the wick to the end. Arrange the candles in a circle around it, beginning with the gold one behind the cauldron and working clockwise. Light the candles in the same order in which you placed them. Say the chant nine times. Leave the candles to burn out completely. Dispose of the wax afterward.

Chant—Life and healing the Goddess (God) brings.

Accept the healing! Welcome the healing!

See Fig. 28, on page 160.

Regain Health

Candles—Straight or votive candles in the following colors: one light blue (inner peace, good health), one brown (balance, grounding) , and one gold (healing, happiness).

Oil—Carnation.

Herbs—Red sandalwood.

Incense—Carnation or rose.

Stones—Bloodstone and boji stones.

Other Supplies—Placket containing a photo or paper with the person's name.

Timing—On the full moon or the waxing moon cycle.

Day—Sunday (health, healing), Thursday (good health), Monday (medicine), or Wednesday (medicine).

Advice—Sometimes, after a person is healed of a disease, he or she still needs to regain lost ground before he or she is totally well again.

Spellwork—Light the altar candles and the incense. Place the placket in the center of the workspace, with a boji stone on each side of it (boji stones always come in pairs), and the bloodstone behind it. Anoint the candles from the wick to the end. Put the brown candle in front of the placket, the light blue one on the left, and the gold one on the right. Light the candles in the same order you arranged them. Say the chant. Leave the candles to burn out completely. Dispose of the wax afterward.

Chant—Strength return to the body.

Peace return to the mind.

Contentment return to the soul.

Balance and energy return to (name)'s life.

See Fig. 29, on page 161.

Recovery from Surgery

Candles—One red figure candle. Straight or votive candles in the following colors: four red (energy, will power, good health), four orange (stamina, encouragement), and four white (balance the aura, raise the vibrations).

Oil—Lilac.

Herbs—Pine needles.

Incense—Cedar or sandalwood.

Stones—Carnelian and boji stones.

Other Supplies—Small nail.

Timing—On the full moon or the waxing moon cycle.

Day—Tuesday.

Advice—Surgery always damages the body's aura, thus leaving it open to potential disease of another kind. This ritual will seal the aura and help the patient to recover faster.

Spellwork—Light the altar candles and the incense. Using the nail, mark the red figure candle in the same place as the surgery, duplicating the site of the scar as closely as possible. If it was a tonsillectomy, mark both sides of the neck. Lay the figure candle in the center of your workspace and lightly rub the boji stones over the mark or marks. Anoint the candles from the wick to the end. Stand the figure upright in the center of your working space and place one boji stone on each side of it. Arrange the white candles at four sides around this figure. (See the diagram.) Next, arrange the orange candles in a square around the white ones. Finish by setting the red candles in a square around the orange ones. Light the figure candles, followed by each square of candles in the same order in which you set them out. Say the chant five times. Leave the candles to burn out completely. Dispose of the wax afterward.

Chant—What was harmed is mended.

What was cut is healed.

What was removed is balanced.

The Light of healing mends all, balances all.

Complete healing is accomplished through
the Light.

See Fig. 30, on page 161.

Purification

Candles—Straight or votive candles in the following colors: one white (purity, spiritual contact), one purple (spirit contact, drive away evil), one silver (remove negative powers), and one gold (higher influences, healing).

Oil—Pine.

Herbs—Rosemary.

Incense—Frankincense, pine, or rosemary.

Stones—Aquamarine and tourmaline.

Other Supplies—None.

Timing—On the full moon or the waxing moon cycle.

Day—Sunday.

Advice—If you have undergone an illness, an extremely emotional experience, been around very negative people, or through a traumatic event, you need to consider using this ritual to purify your aura. Negative experiences of any kind frequently leave a number of very small holes in the aura, which open you up to even more negative experiences.

Spellwork—Light the altar candles and the incense. Anoint the candles from the wick to the end. Set the candles out in a zigzag line, like a lightning bolt laid horizontally on your altar. Place the candles in this order, beginning on the left: white, purple, silver, and gold. Set the aquamarine to the left of the white candle and the tourmaline to the right of the gold one. Light the candles in the same order you arranged them. Say the chant. Leave the candles to burn out completely. Dispose of the wax afterward.

Chant—Swift as lightning, pure Love and Light flow
      through my body.

All negatives are burned away in this universal
power.
Willingly, I stand before this altar as a cleaned vessel,
Waiting for the inflow of positive energy.

See Fig. 31, on page 162.

Banish Serious or Terminal Illness

Candles—Black skull candle, astrological candle for the person for whom the healing is being done.

Oil—Myrrh or patchouli.

Herbs—Rue.

Incense—Frankincense, combined frankincense and myrrh, patchouli, or vervain.

Stones—Black obsidian and black onyx.

Other Supplies—Small nail.

Timing—On the new moon or during the waning moon cycle.

Day—Saturday.

Advice—As with any healing, make certain the sick person actually wants to recover. If she/he feels that her/his time has come, do not interfere with karma, but instead work for a peaceful passing.

Spellwork—Light the altar candles and the incense. Using a nail or other sharp instrument, carve the sick person's name and the name of her/his disease onto the black skull candle. Carve only the person's initials on the astrological candle. Anoint the skull candle from the end to the wick, the astrological candle from the wick to the end. In the center of the altar, place the skull candle and an astrological candle representing the sick person, side by side, touching. Place the onyx and obsidian near the skull candle.

Light the skull candle first, then the astrological candle. While concentrating on the sick person, say the chant. Leave the candles burning. The skull candle will burn longer than the astrological candle, so you must have others ready. Just before the astrological candle burns out, light another astrological candle. An astrological candle must be burning at all times until the skull candle is completely burned out.

Each day move the candles one inch farther apart until the skull candle is burned out or they reach the farthest points on the altar. Each time you move the candles, repeat the chant. If the candles are still burning after you have moved them as far as you can, leave them there until the skull candle is out. Dispose of all the wax.

If, at the end of this process, the skull candle has burned out only the inside, leaving an outer shell, the threat remains. You will have to repeat the candle spell.

Chant—Be gone, you darkened specter.

Be gone, all illness and fear.

Healing and Light only may come.

This I declare, for one full year.

See Fig. 32, on page 162.

LOVE

Stop Interference in Your Love or Marriage

Candles—A red and black double-action candle. Straight or votive candles in the following colors: one black (bind negative forces, break up blockages), one light blue (inner peace, harmony), and one indigo (stop another's actions).

Oil—Frangipani.

Herbs—Bay laurel.

Incense—Frangipani or pine.

Stones—Moonstone, chrysocolla, and pyrite.

Other Supplies—A small steel or iron nail.

Timing—On the full moon or during the waxing moon.

Day—Friday.

Advice—Interference may come in the form of family, friends, or outsiders. Decisions must be made by the couple about continuing a relationship with the offending parties if they will not cease their interference.

Spellwork—Light the altar candles and the incense. Using the nail, carve two hearts into the red portion of the candle; put your initials inside one heart, your lover's initials inside the other. Then stick the nail into the candle where the red wax meets the black wax. Anoint the black candle from the end to the wick; the others from the wick to the end. Set the black candle behind the double-action candle, with the pyrite behind it. Set the light blue candle and the moonstone on the left of the double-action candle and the indigo candle and the chrysocolla on the right. Light the double-action candle first, then the other candles. Say the chant. Burn the double-action candle down to the nail. Allow the other candles to burn out completely. Then dispose of the central candle and all wax from the others.

Chant—No one can come between us.

> The troublemakers receive back their own
> words and actions.

We walk only in the Light.

See Fig. 33, on page 163.

Heal an Unhappy Marriage or Relationship

Candles—Straight or votive candles in the following colors: two green (good fortune, balance, marriage), two gold (happiness), and two pink (true love, honor).

Oil—Rose.

Herbs—Rose petals or yarrow.

Incense—Apple blossom, allspice, or sandalwood.

Stones—Agate, amethyst, and lapis lazuli.

Other Supplies—Small nail.

Timing—On the full moon or the waxing moon cycle.

Day—Friday.

Advice—Healing an unhappy relationship may come in many forms. It may mean that all differences are resolved, or one partner must continue to endure the situation because the other will not change. Or, it may mean that separation is the only healing that can come to a troubled partnership.

Spellwork—Light the altar candles and the incense. Using a nail, inscribe each of the green candles with initials of one member of the couple. Anoint all the candles from the wick to the end. Set them side by side in the center of your working space. Behind them, place one gold candle, with the stones in a vertical line behind the gold candle. Place the other gold candle before the green candles. One pink candle is set on the right, and the other on the left. Light the green candles first, then the other candles. Say the chant. Leave the candles to burn out completely. Dispose of the wax afterward.

Chant—All that was broken is mended.

      All that was wrong is made right.

      All darkness and hurt are banished.

      All that remains is the Light.

See Fig. 34, on page 163.

Win the Love of a Man

Candles—Straight or votive candles in the following colors: one red male figure candle (physical desire, love), two gold (happiness, fast luck), and two white (sincerity, spirituality).

Oil—Vanilla.

Herbs—Catnip or ginger.

Incense—Vanilla or ylang-ylang.

Stones—Lodestone, aventurine, and malachite.

Other Supplies—Small nail; small piece of paper.

Timing—On the full moon or the waxing moon cycle.

Day—Friday.

Advice—Do not use this spell to force someone to love you. Control over another will only bring you heartache and misery. The controlled person will always resent your action subconsciously and will constantly try to move away from you. This spell is best used when a person is in love with you, but is hesitant to make a commitment.

Spellwork—Light the altar candles and the incense. Using a nail, carve the initials of the man into the red figure candle. Write your name on the piece of paper. Anoint all the candles from the wick to the end, and set the figure candle in the center of your workspace. Place a gold (on the outside) and a white candle to both the left and right of this figure. Put the aventurine between the left-hand candles, and the malachite between the right-hand ones. Set the lodestone behind the figure candle and on the paper containing your name. Light the figure candle first, then the others. Say the chant seven times. Leave the candles to burn out completely. Dispose of the wax after the figure candle has burned out.

Chant—Love and warmth I offer thee.

Hear me, lover. Come to me.

See Fig. 35, on page 164.

Win the Love of a Woman

Candles—Straight or votive candles in the following colors: one red female figure candle (physical desire, love), two silver (help from feminine deities), and two white (sincerity, spirituality).

Oil—Rose.

Herbs—Rose petals.

Incense—Frangipani or rose.

Stones—Coral, lodestone, and rose quartz.

Other Supplies—Small nail, small piece of paper.

Timing—On the full moon or the waxing moon cycle.

Day—Friday.

Advice—See the advice on the previous spell.

Spellwork—Light the altar candles and the incense. Using a nail, carve the initials of the woman into the red figure candle. Write your name on the piece of paper. Anoint all the candles from the wick to the end, and set the figure candle in the center of your workspace. Place a silver and a white (on the outside) candle to both the left and right of this figure. Put the coral between the left-hand candles, and the rose quartz between the right-hand ones. Set the lodestone behind the figure candle and on the paper containing your name. Light the figure candle first, then the others. Say the chant seven times. Leave the candles to burn out completely. Dispose of the wax after the figure candle has burned out.

Chant—Love and protection I offer thee.

Hear me, lover. Come to me.

See Fig. 36, on page 164.

Find the Perfect Mate

Candles—A red seven-knob candle, plus seven straight or votive candles in the following colors: light blue (inner peace, harmony), green (good fortune, marriage), indigo (balance out karma), orange (success, energy), pink (true love, romance), and white (sincerity, purity).

Oil—Musk.

Herbs—Rue.

Incense—Musk or patchouli.

Stones—Moss agate, clear quartz crystal, lapis lazuli, and rose quartz.

Other Supplies—Small piece of paper with your name on it.

Timing—On the full moon or the waxing moon cycle.

Day—Monday or Friday.

Advice—This love spell is the safest and best to use, as it does not target any particular individual. Instead, it reaches out into the universe to bring you the best and perfect mate for you.

Spellwork—Light the altar candles and the incense. Anoint the candles from the wick to the end. Place the red seven-knob candle in the center of your altar workplace. Set the other candles in a spiral around the red candle, beginning with the light blue on the inside in front of the seven-knob candle and ending with the white on the outer end of the spiral. Place the paper containing your name next to the white candle. Put the stones, one at each side, around the paper. (See the diagram.) First, light the red candle, then the others. Say the chant three times. Extinguish all the candles when the red candle has burned one knob. Relight all the candles at the same time each night for seven nights and repeat the chant each time. The last night, leave the candles to burn out completely. Dispose of the wax afterward.

Chant—One to seek her/him, one to find her/him.

One to bring her/him, one to bind her/him.

Heart to heart, forever one.

So say I, this spell is done.

See Fig. 37, on page 165.

Release an Unwanted Admirer or Lover

Candles—Two red figure candles, the sexes representing the sexes of the two people involved.

Oil—Patchouli.

Herbs—Lemon verbena.

Incense—Patchouli or rue.

Stones—Spectrolite, jade, clear quartz crystal, agate, and malachite.

Other Supplies—Small nail.

Timing—On the new moon or the waning moon cycle.

Day—Tuesday.

Advice—Sometimes you find yourself in a relationship, friendship, or situation with a person that is not good for you. It can be a problem to get possessive people to let go. This spell will make it easier to move them out of your surroundings. However, you must do your part by calmly stating, if possible, that the relationship or friendship is ended, and that you are definitely not interested.

Spellwork—Light the altar candles and the incense. Using a nail, carve the appropriate initials into each figure candle. Anoint the candles from the wick to the end. Place the figure candles back to back on the altar. Place the clear quartz crystal between the two figures. Set the spectrolite centered behind the figures, the agate on the left, the jade on the right, and the malachite in front of them. Light the candles. Say the chant nine times. Burn the candles for one hour each day. Each day, move the figures farther apart, still facing away from each other. On the last day, leave the candles to burn out completely. Dispose of the wax.

Chant—Peacefully, we walk away.

No pain or sorrow remain.

Separately, we live our lives,

Never to join again.

See Fig. 38, on page 165.

PROTECTION

Stop Slander and Gossip

Candles—A black and white double-action candle, plus straight or votive candles in the following colors: one black (remove negative energies) and one indigo (stop gossip and lies).

Oil—Juniper or lilac.

Herbs—Clove or marjoram.

Incense—Cypress or pine.

Stones—Aquamarine, hematite, and agate.

Other Supplies—A small nail; piece of shiny foil.

Timing—During a waning moon.

Day—Tuesday.

Advice—Although this spell will stop gossip, you must remain alert that by your actions and words you do not set up another situation that will bring more gossip your way. Also, do not gossip yourself.

Spellwork—Light the altar candles and the incense. With the nail, carve an eye inside a triangle on the white part of the candle. Anoint the black candle from the end to the wick; the others from the wick to the end. Then stick the nail into the double-action candle right where the black wax starts. Place the candle on shiny foil and light it. Put the stones around the candle. Set the black candle on the left of the double-action candle and the indigo one on the right; light them. As the white wax drips down and covers the black wax, the gossip will return to the one who sent it. Say the chant three times. Burn the candle down to the nail. Then dispose of the candle and all wax from it.

Chant—Your mouth is stopped.

Your eyes see naught.

Your thoughts are bound.

Your words turn 'round.

No longer will you bother me.

This is my will. So shall it be.

See Fig. 39, on page 166.

Rid Yourself of Negatives

Candles—Straight or votive candles in the following colors: one black (remove negative energies, protection), one light blue (inner peace, harmony, contacting the Higher Self), one brown (balance, grounding), and one magenta (exorcism, healing, fast action).

Oil—Pine.

Herbs—Basil.

Incense—Cedar or vervain.

Stones—Two pieces each of hematite and smoky quartz.

Other Supplies—Placket with your photo.

Timing—On the new moon or the waning moon cycle.

Day—Tuesday or Saturday.

Advice—Ridding yourself of negatives may require you to give up certain friends, activities, and habits. Think carefully about this before performing this ritual.

Spellwork—Light the altar candles and the incense. Place the placket containing your photo in the center of your workspace. Put a piece of hematite behind and in front of the placket, with a piece of smoky quartz on each side. Anoint the black candle from the end to the wick; the others from the wick to the end. Set the black candle behind the placket, with the light blue on the right side, the brown in front, and the magenta on the left. Light the candles in the same order as you arranged them. Say the chant five times. Leave the candles to burn out completely. Dispose of the wax afterward.

Chant—All negatives go out of my life.
　　　　Only positive enters.
　　　　I turn from the path of darkness,
　　　　And walk only in the way of Light.
　　　　I am cleansed. I am purified. I am changed.
See Fig. 40, on page 166.

Binding Troublesome People

Candles—Straight or votive candles in the following colors:
one black (cause confusion to enemies, protection) and one
purple (drive away evil, spiritual protection).

Oil—Patchouli.

Herbs—Patchouli.

Incense—Cypress or pine.

Stones—Jade, lapis lazuli, and two pieces of black onyx.

Other Supplies—A small metal cauldron; a small piece of paper.

Timing—On the new moon or the waning moon cycle.

Day—Saturday.

Advice—Sometimes nice little spells simply do not make an
impression on certain types of malicious, harmful people. Then
you must be willing to do whatever is required to protect yourself from harassment, revenge, or whatever nasty tactics are
being used. Binding them, or preventing them from doing mis-
chief, is one way to protect yourself.

Spellwork—Light the altar candles and the incense. Put the
cauldron in the center of your workspace. If you know for

certain the names of the offending people, write them on the paper. If you are unsure, simply write "all my enemies." Place the paper inside the cauldron. Anoint the black candle from the end to the wick; the purple from the wick to the end. Set the black candle to the left of the cauldron, the purple candle to the right. Place the lapis lazuli behind the cauldron and the jade in front of it, with one piece of black onyx on the right side of the cauldron and another piece on the left of the cauldron. Light the candles and say the chant slowly five times. After the candles are burned completely out, burn the paper with the names. Dispose of the wax and ashes.

Chant—Darkness is ended.

Interference is done.

Enemies are shackled.

My battle is won.

See Fig. 41, on page 167.

Release One from Enthrallment

Candles—A separation candle, which is a large red jumbo candle dipped completely in black. Straight or votive candles in the following colors: one purple (break bad luck, influence people), one white (power of a higher nature, truth), and two orange (sudden changes, success).

Oil—Cedar or dragon's blood.

Herbs—Dragon's blood.

Incense—Patchouli or myrrh.

Stones—Chalcedony, tourmaline, and malachite.

Other Supplies—Small nail.

Timing—On the new moon or the waning moon cycle.

Day—Tuesday.

Advice—The only time this break-up spell is justified is when a loved one is being hurt by the person with whom he/she has a relationship. This can be a daughter who is involved with an abuser, alcoholic, or drug addict, or a family member who is blind to one who is conning him/her out of his/her money and possessions.

Spellwork—Light the altar candles and the incense. Using a nail, carve the initials of the enthralled person into the separation candle. Anoint the candles from the wick to the end. Place the separation candle in the center of your working space, with the purple candle on the left and the white candle on the right, with an orange candle behind and in front. Put the chalcedony behind the separation candle with the malachite on the right and the tourmaline on the left. Light the separation candle first, then the other candles. Say the chant slowly three times. Leave the candles to burn out completely. Dispose of the wax afterward.

Chant—All that was joined is now severed.

All that was wrong is now right.

All that was shadowed is brightness.

The truth is revealed by the Light.

See Fig. 42, on page 167.

Release from Psychic Attack or Ill-Wishing

Candles—A purple (drive away evil, spiritual protection) seven-knob candle (or seven purple straight or votive candles), plus seven each of the colors black (absorb and remove negative energies), indigo (neutralize the magic of others), and white (spiritual protection).

Oil—Patchouli or frankincense.

Herbs—Patchouli.

Incense—Cedar or myrrh.

Stones—Smoky quartz, turquoise, and black obsidian.

Other Supplies—Small nail.

Timing—On the new moon or the waning moon cycle.

Day—Saturday.

Advice—Psychic attack is usually perpetrated knowingly by people, while ill-wishing is the continual repeating of negative statements to you or about you. Both can cause all kinds of problems. These energies should be returned to their senders.

Spellwork—Light the altar candles and the incense. Carve your initials into the purple seven-knob candle with a nail, anoint it from the wick to the end, and set it in the center of your workspace. Anoint the black candle from the end to the wick; the others from the wick to the end. Place the black candle and the black obsidian behind the seven-knob candle. Set the white candle and the clear quartz crystal on the right side, and the indigo candle and the turquoise on the left. Light the seven-knob candle, then the other candles. Say the chant seven times. Burn only one knob of the purple candle each night. Leave the other candles to burn out completely. Use fresh black, indigo, and white candles each night. Dispose of the wax afterward.

Chant—All evil returns to the maker and source.
　　　　　　The rebound hits with a tenfold force.
　　　　　　My enemies have no power o'er me.
　　　　　　As I will, so shall it be!

See Fig. 43, on page 168.

Remove Negative Vibrations or Spirits from a Home

Candles—A purple (drive away evil, spiritual protection) seven-knob candle (or seven purple straight or votive candles), plus seven each of the colors black (absorb and remove negative energies), royal blue (happiness, calling upon occult power), and magenta (fast action, exorcism).

Oil—Vetiver or yarrow.

Herbs—Vervain or patchouli.

Incense—Frankincense, myrrh, or patchouli.

Stones—Agate, clear quartz crystal, and bloodstone.

Other Supplies—Holy water. Bless water yourself in full moonlight by asking Goddess/God to make it pure, or see if you can obtain it from any Catholic Church.

Timing—On the new moon or the waning moon cycle.

Day—Saturday or Tuesday.

Advice—Negative vibrations or a spirit may already occupy a house or apartment when you move in, especially if a previous occupant was troubled in spirit or led a negative lifestyle. These forces can range from mildly irritating to outright disruptive and dangerous. It is a good idea to cleanse any new place of residence, or recleanse your present dwelling place on a monthly basis. On rare occasions, an earthbound, dangerous spirit will require an expert to remove it.

Spellwork—Light the altar candles and the incense. Anoint the black candle from the end to the wick; the others from the wick to the end. Place the seven-knob candle in the center of your altar workspace. Set the black candle and the bloodstone behind the seven-knob candle, with the magenta candle and agate on the right side, and the royal blue candle and clear quartz crystal on the left. Light the seven-knob candle first, then the others. Say the chant nine times. Take the bottle of holy water and sprinkle each corner of every room in the house or apartment, ending up at the front door. Open the door and order the spirit or vibrations to leave at once. Then close the door and sprinkle it also. Burn only one knob of the central candle each night. Leave the other candles on the altar to burn out completely, replacing them with fresh candles each night. Dispose of the wax afterward.

Chant—This is a place of Light and Love.
No darkness or evil can remain here.
By the power of the Goddess (God),
I order all darkness to leave at once!
Out with the darkness! In with the Light!

See Fig. 44, on page 168.

Remove Negative Vibrations or Spirits from a Person

Candles—A purple (drive away evil, spiritual protection) seven-knob candle (or seven purple straight or votive candles), plus seven each of the colors black (absorb and remove negative energies), royal blue (happiness, calling upon occult power), magenta (fast action, exorcism), and silver (neutralize negative powers, repel destructive forces).

Oil—Vetiver or patchouli.

Herbs—Vervain or patchouli.

Incense—Frankincense, myrrh, or patchouli.

Stones—Agate, clear quartz crystal, black onyx, and black obsidian.

Other Supplies—Holy water; small nail.

Timing—On the new moon or the waning moon cycle.

Day—Saturday or Tuesday.

Advice—Determining personal possession can be a tricky decision. Some types of temporary or permanent mental illness can be mistaken for possession. So can certain types of willful behavior. If you are uncertain, consult an expert in the field. At no time should you ever use force of any kind to exorcise a person or inflict any type of physical or mental punishment!

Spellwork—Light the altar candles and the incense. Using a nail, carve the initials of the troubled person into the purple seven-knob candle. Anoint it from the wick to the end and place it in the center of your altar workspace. Anoint the black candle from the end to the wick; the others from the wick to the end. Place the black candle and the black obsidian behind the seven-knob candle, with the magenta candle and agate on the right side, the silver candle and the black onyx in front of it, and the royal blue candle and clear quartz crystal on the left. Say the chant seven times as you sprinkle the "possessed" person with the holy water. Even though this spell may appear to work the first time you do it, repeat it for the remaining six nights. Each night burn only one knob of the purple candle. Leave the other candles to burn out completely, replacing them with fresh candles each night. Dispose of the wax afterward.

Chant—By the power of Light, I cast out all evil and
darkness.

By the power of Light, I call upon only goodness
to dwell in this body.

By the power of the Goddess (God), I set you free!

See Fig. 45, on page 169.

Bring Pressure to Bear on an Enemy

Candles—A purple seven-knob candle (or seven purple straight or votive candles), plus seven each of indigo (balance out karma, stop another's actions) and magenta (fast action, spiritual healing).

Oil—Pine.

Herbs—Bay laurel or clove.

Incense—Dragon's blood, pine, or patchouli.

Stones—Aquamarine.

Other Supplies—Small nail.

Timing—During a waning moon.

Day—Saturday or Tuesday.

Advice—Sometimes the only way to stop enemies is to put them under pressure from their own lives. Then they have no time to worry about you.

Spellwork—Light the altar candles and the incense. With a nail, carve the initials or name of the enemy into the purple seven-knob candle. Anoint the candles from the wick to the end. Place the aquamarine in front of the seven-knob candle with the indigo candle on the left and the magenta one on the right. Light the seven-knob candle first, then the others. Say the chant. Sit quietly and visualize yourself building a thick stone wall between you and your enemy. Take your time with this, for when you can feel that this wall is there, your protection will be complete. Everything negative sent to you will rebound upon the sender. Each night burn only one knob of the purple candle. Leave the other candles to burn out completely, replacing them with fresh candles each night. Dispose of the wax afterward.

Chant—One to seek her/him. One to find her/him.

One to bring her/him. One to bind her/him.

Stone to stone, forever one.

So say I. This spell is done.

See Fig. 46, on page 169.

Uncross a Person

Candles—A black seven-knob candle (or seven black straight or votive candles), plus seven each of royal blue (occult power), magenta (exorcism, fast action), purple (drive away evil, remove hexes), and silver (neutralize negative powers).

Oil—Cedar or patchouli.

Herbs—Dragon's blood or wormwood.

Incense—Cedar, myrrh, or patchouli.

Stones—Holey stone, mica, clear quartz crystal, black obsidian, black onyx, and sard.

Other Supplies—Placket with photo; holy water. To make or obtain holy water, see the "Remove Negative Vibrations from a Person" spell.

Timing—On the new moon or the waning moon cycle.

Day—Saturday.

Advice—Active hexing or putting a magical curse on a person is vastly different from ill-wishing someone. Hexing is a willful act, requiring thought and determination. This can have devastating effects on the life of the person hexed, such as loss of job and money, a turn of ill health, trouble in relationships, and any number of other negative occurrences. To remove a hex, it requires seven nights (preferably at midnight) and deep concentration and determination on the part of the hexed person and the person helping.

Spellwork—Light the altar candles and the incense. Anoint the black candle from the end to the wick, the others from the wick to the end. Place the placket containing the photo of the hexed person in the center of your workspace. In front of it set the black seven-knob candle with the black obsidian on the left and the black onyx on the right. Put the purple candle behind the placket, and the silver one in front of the black seven-knob candle. Set the royal blue candle to the left of the seven-knob candle with the magenta one to the right. Place the remaining stones, one beside each of these last candles. Light the seven-knob candle first, then the other candles. Say the chant as you sprinkle the hexed person with holy water. Each night burn only one knob of the black candle. Leave the other candles to burn out completely, replacing them with fresh candles each night. Dispose of the wax afterward.

Chant—Power of the Light, come to my call!

> Release (name) from bondage of this curse.
> Return it tenfold to the sender.
> Fill (name) with the holy power of Light!

See Fig. 47, on page 170.

Protect Someone from Abuse

Candles—Straight or votive candles in the following colors: one white (confidence, mental clarity, spiritual healing), one purple (protection, break bad luck, break influence of others), one black (creates confusion for enemies, unsticks stagnant situations, removes negative energies), and one pink (affection, banish depression).

Oil—Frankincense.

Herbs—Bay laurel or frankincense.

Incense—Dragon's blood, frankincense, or patchouli.

Stones—Jasper, lapis lazuli, smoky quartz, and black obsidian.

Other Supplies—Small nail.

Timing—On the new moon or the waning moon cycle.

Day—Tuesday.

Advice—Although this spell will help protect the victim, she/he must eventually make a decision to move out of the situation.

Spellwork—Light the altar candles and the incense. Using the nail, carve the name or initials of the abuser into the black candle and the name or initials of the victim into the white candle. Anoint the black candle from wick to the end, the other candles from the end to the wick. Arrange the candles in a straight line on your workspace, with the pink on the left, white next, followed by the purple candle. Set the black candle to the far right away from the other candles. Place the jasper behind the pink candle, the lapis lazuli behind the white, and the smoky quartz crystal behind to the purple. The black obsidian goes behind the distant black candle. Light the three candles to the left, then the black one. Say the chant. Visualize the black candle moving farther and farther away until its flame is only a tiny spot of light. Leave the candles to burn out completely. Dispose of the wax afterward.

Chant—Change anger to calmness, darkness to light,
       Turn (abuser's name) to love, his/her path to
       what's right.

Protect those around him/her. Fill all with peace.
Fill all with healing. Let all violence cease.

See Fig. 48, on page 170.

SPIRITUALITY

Communicate with Spirit

Candles—Straight or votive candles in the following colors: one royal blue (occult power, expansion), one indigo (meditation, balances out karma), one magenta (spiritual healing), one purple (higher psychic ability, spirit contact), and one white (purity, contact spirit helpers).

Oil—Yarrow or frankincense and myrrh.

Herbs—Lavender.

Incense—Frankincense or lotus.

Stones—Amethyst, emerald, labradorite, moonstone, and sugilite.

Other Supplies—None.

Timing—On the full moon or the waxing moon cycle.

Day—Monday.

Advice—The most perfect communications with Spirit come through meditation and prayer. If you call upon the Light before you do each meditation, and open yourself to what is right, not merely what you want to hear, you will have no problem making a firm and truthful contact with the spiritual realm.

Spellwork—Light the altar candles and the incense. Anoint all of the candles from the wick to the end. Place the white candle in the center of your working space on the altar. Behind it, set the purple candle, with the magenta to the right, the royal blue in front of it, and the indigo to the left. Put the labradorite behind the purple candle, the moonstone to the right of the magenta, the sugilite in front of the royal blue, and the amethyst to the left of the indigo one. Light the white candle first, then the surrounding ones. Say the chant. Leave the candles to burn out completely. Dispose of the wax afterward. Watch your dreams for spiritual communications.

Chant—Open the doors to Spirit wide.
> Take my hand and guide me inside.
> Let me know the great wisdom, the strength,
> and the love,
> That comes from sweet blending with Spirit above.

See Fig. 49, on page 171.

Meet Your Spirit Guide

Candles—Straight or votive candles in the following colors: one royal blue (occult power), one purple (higher influences, intuition), and one white (contact spirit helpers, raise the vibrations).

Oil—Honeysuckle.

Herbs—Mugwort.

Incense—Sandalwood or lotus.

Stones—Moss agate, lapis lazuli, moonstone, sugilite, and tourmaline.

Other Supplies—Small mirror large enough to reflect most of your face.

Timing—On the full moon or the waxing moon cycle.

Day—Monday.

Advice—The mistake most people make when contacting spirit guides is to assume that they will get some great magician or high teacher. The majority of people on the earth are the common people. They are the ones who actually make things run right, not the big officials in some decorated office. If you want true wisdom and aid, ask for some knowledgeable, striving teacher who can help you with everyday problems. Common sense, grassroots wisdom can beat out an over-puffed ego every time.

Spellwork—Light the altar candles and the incense. Set the mirror upright in the center of your workspace. Anoint all the candles from the wick to the end. Set the purple candle with the sugilite behind it behind the mirror. Place the white candle with the lapis lazuli outside to the right, and the royal blue one with the tourmaline outside to the left. To finish, put the moonstone by the left corner of the mirror and the agate by the right corner. Light the candles and look into the mirror as you say the chant. Watch for subtle changes in your appearance or flickers of movement in the mirror. These are signs that a teacher or teachers are present. Leave the candles to burn out completely. Dispose of the wax afterward.

Chant—I knock upon the spiritual door
        In search of guidance, knowledge, more.
        I seek to know who walks with me.
        This I do will. So shall it be.
See Fig. 50, on page 171.

Enhance Spiritual Growth

Candles—Straight or votive candles in the following colors: white (purity, balance the aura), royal blue (expansion, occult power), and gold (intuition, higher influences). Six votive candles to represent the chakras: red, orange, yellow, green, blue, and lavender.

Oil—Lotus.

Herbs—Frankincense.

Incense—Lotus or sandalwood.

Stones—Amber, citrine, lapis lazuli, ruby, and sapphire.

Other Supplies—None.

Timing—On the full moon or the waxing moon cycle.

Day—Monday.

Advice—To enhance spiritual growth, all your chakras must be working in a proper manner. The six colored votive candles plus the larger white candle represent the seven chakras each person has in her/his astrological body. This candle spell will help to correct any imbalances in the chakras, thus making a firmer connection with the spiritual.

Spellwork—Light the altar candles and the incense. Anoint all the candles from the wick to the end. To the back center of your workspace, set the white candle with the lapis lazuli behind it. Place the gold candle with the amber behind it to the right, and the royal blue candle with the sapphire behind it to the left. Place the citrine between the blue and white candles, and the ruby between the white and gold ones. Arrange the votive candles in a vertical line in this order leading up to the white candle—red the closest to you, followed by orange, yellow, green, blue, and lavender. Light the three larger upper candles first. Then light the chakra candles, beginning with the red and ending with the lavender. Say the chant. Leave the candles to burn out completely. Dispose of the wax afterward.

Chant—I seek only the Light.
> May it fill my life and soul with goodness.
> May it bless me in all ways, leading me only in
>   paths of Light.
> I sincerely ask the Goddess (God) to open my heart
>   to spiritual growth.

See Fig. 51, on page 172.

Gain Spiritual Blessings

Candles—Straight or votive candles in the following colors: one white (balance the aura, wholeness), gold (higher influences, healing, happiness), magenta (balance out karma), and one purple (spiritual protection and healing).

Oil—Frankincense.

Herbs—Frankincense.

Incense—Frankincense or lotus.

Stones—Amethyst, lapis lazuli, moldavite, and black tourmaline.

Other Supplies—A spiritual symbol that has meaning for you.

Timing—On the full moon or the waxing moon cycle.

Day—Monday.

Advice—This spell not only creates an inflow of spiritual blessings, but it will also aid you in completing any karmic ties you have with others. Although this is desirable, it can be difficult, especially when relationships fall apart or your whole life undergoes a change. Be very certain you are willing to undergo any of this before you do this spell.

Spellwork—Light the altar candles and the incense. Place the spiritual symbol in the center of your working space. Anoint all the candles from the wick to the end. Arrange the purple candle to the upper left of the symbol with the moldavite above it. Set the white candle at the upper right with the lapis lazuli above it. Place the gold candle at the lower left of the symbol with the amethyst below it, and the magenta candle at the lower right with the black tourmaline below it. Say the chant. Leave the candles to burn out completely. Dispose of the wax afterward. Place the symbol where you can see it every day.

Chant—Blessings I seek to better my life,

        To chase away darkness, diminish the strife,

To heal me in body, my mind, and my soul.

This I request. This is my goal.

See Fig. 52, on page 172.

Strengthen Your Psychic Abilities

Candles—Straight or votive candles in the following colors: one purple (higher psychic ability), one white (purity, wholeness, balance the aura), and one silver (develop psychic abilities).

Oil—Jasmine.

Herbs—Wormwood or jasmine flowers.

Incense—Honeysuckle, mimosa, or lotus.

Stones—Moss agate, moonstone, jet, blue topaz, and purple tourmaline.

Other Supplies—Small bag that can be tightly closed.

Timing—On the full moon or the waxing moon cycle.

Day—Monday.

Advice—There are a wide variety of psychic abilities. Do not get caught up in the idea that you have to do something flashy or go out and do readings for other people. Using the psychic to read for others is a very physically and emotionally draining experience. Instead, you should desire to cultivate your psychic abilities to make a better life for yourself.

Spellwork—Light the altar candles and the incense. Anoint all the candles from the wick to the end. Place the bag in the center of your altar working space. Set the purple candle to the left of the bag with the purple tourmaline above it. Put the white candle to the right of the bag with the moonstone above it. Place the silver candle below the bag with the jet in front of it. The agate is placed between the silver and purple candles, while the topaz goes between the silver and white candles. Say the chant. Place the stones into the bag. Carry the bag with you, or sleep with it under your pillow. Leave the candles to burn out completely. Dispose of the wax afterward.

Chant—Open my soul's eye that sees all beyond
This earthly plane and into the Light.
Teach me to listen, to reach out with my intuition.
This is my spiritual heritage. Help me to use it
wisely.

See Fig. 53, on page 173.

Prepare for Divination

Candles—Straight or votive candles in the following colors: one purple (spirit contact, divination), one white (purity, balance the aura, raise the vibrations), one silver (develop psychic abilities, raise the vibrations), and one light blue (wisdom, harmony, contacting the Higher Self).

Oil—Honeysuckle or myrrh.

Herbs—Orris root.

Incense—Wisteria or lavender.

Stones—Amethyst, fluorite, moonstone, and clear quartz crystal.

Other Supplies—Whatever divination tools, such as tarot cards or runes, you plan to use.

Timing—On the full moon or the waxing moon cycle.

Day—Wednesday or Monday.

Advice—Skill in any form of divination takes practice. This spell will help you open more easily to spiritual aid.

Spellwork—Light the altar candles and the incense. Arrange the divination tool in the center of your altar space. Anoint all of the candles from the wick to the end. Place the white candle at the upper left of the altar with the moonstone to the left. Put the silver candle at the upper right of the altar with the clear quartz crystal to its right. The purple candle goes below the white candle with the amethyst to its left, while the light blue candle goes below the silver candle with the fluorite to its right. By situating the candles in this manner, you can safely practice your divination in the center without disturbing the candles. Say the chant. Then do whatever divination method you planned. Leave the candles to burn out completely. Dispose of the wax afterward.

Chant—Unlock the secret inner door. Give to me the key
    That reveals the aged secrets. Let me the future see.
    Grant wisdom for enlightenment, understanding, more.
    Sweet Spirit, lead me inward to the hidden sacred door.

See Fig. 54, on page 173.

Enhance Your Dreams and Find Guidance

Candles—Straight or votive candles in the following colors: one light blue (truth, inspiration, wisdom), one brown (ESP, balance, intuition), and one pink (spiritual awakening and healing).

Oil—Jasmine or sage.

Herbs—Marigold.

Incense—Frankincense or jasmine.

Stones—Agate, amethyst, jade, and clear quartz crystal.

Other Supplies—Small bag with a secure closure.

Timing—On the full moon or the waxing moon cycle.

Day—Monday.

Advice—Learning to interpret dreams is difficult, since no dream book will actually help much. What a cat means to one person may not mean the same to another. You need to use a notebook to record your dreams. Study these dreams and what occurs in life after you have them. Only in this way can you figure out what your subconscious mind is telling you in the symbols it uses, for symbols are the only language that the subconscious mind knows.

Spellwork—Light the altar candles and the incense. Anoint the candles from the wick to the end. Place the bag to the center back of your workspace with the amethyst behind it. Arrange the remaining candles in a straight horizontal line in front of the bag with the stones in front of them: the light blue candle and agate on the left, the brown candle and clear quartz crystal in the middle, and the pink candle and jade on the right. Say the chant. Place the stones in the little bag and sleep with it under your pillow each night. Leave the candles to burn out completely. Dispose of the wax afterward.

Chant—Dreams of mystery, dreams of light,

Come to me softly, sweetly, tonight.

Give to me guidance to help find my way

Through the problems of life that surface each day.

See Fig. 55, on page 174.

Strengthen Your Psychic Shield

Candles—Straight or votive candles in the following colors: one black (absorbs and removes negatives, creates confusion in enemies), two purple (drive away evil, spiritual protection), two white (purity, truth, wholeness), and two silver (develop psychic abilities, remove negative powers).

Oil—Yarrow, sage, or lotus.

Herbs—Peppermint.

Incense—Lotus, patchouli, or sandalwood.

Stones—Two tektite or meteorite, and two tourmaline.

Other Supplies—None.

Timing—On the full moon or the waxing moon cycle.

Day—Sunday.

Advice—A strong psychic shield over your astrological body will keep you from inadvertently picking up negative thought-forms from others with whom you come in contact. If you work around many people, it is a good idea to repeat this ritual once a month during the waxing moon.

Spellwork—Light the altar candles and the incense. Place the black candle in the center of your altar space with one piece of tourmaline to the upper left of it, the other piece to the lower right. Place one tektite or meteorite to the upper right of the black candle, the other piece to the lower left. Arrange one purple candle behind the black one, with the other purple candle before it. Place the white candles, one to the upper right, the other on the lower left. Put one silver candle to the upper left of the black candle, the other on the lower right. Say the chant. Spend a minimum of five minutes visualizing yourself covered with a shining silver-blue suit of armor. Leave the candles to burn out completely. Dispose of the wax afterward.

Chant—By full moon in blackened sky,
      I am not alone. My help is nigh.
      Strong armor shields me. I am free,
      Of all evil and harm that threatens me.
      My shield is of Light, my song is of love.
      My protection is strong for it comes from above.
      My strength never falters. My faith sets me free.
      So I do say, and so shall it be!

See Fig. 56, on page 174.

Afterword

Once you begin the practice of candle magic and see its results for yourself, you will find that you use this simple magical method quite often. Candle burning aids in releasing tension and stress over situations you find difficult to resolve through ordinary actions. It gives you a sense of empowerment and control, which in turn will help you feel better about yourself. When you are more confident, life runs more smoothly.

You need not limit yourself to the chants or spells given in this book. Write your own chants to express what you want. Create the spells that are needed in your life. And realize that there are no boundaries to what you can achieve with candle-burning magic.

ILLUSTRATIONS OF CANDLE ALTARS

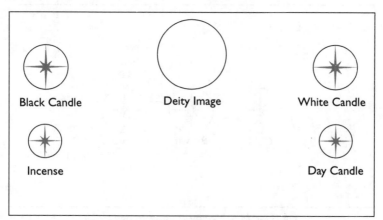

Fig. 1 General Altar (See text, page 68.)

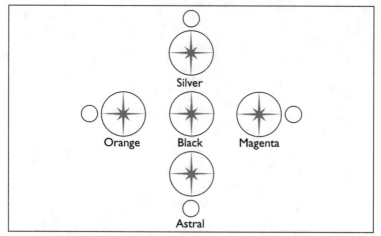

Fig. 2 Change Your Luck (See text, page 70.)

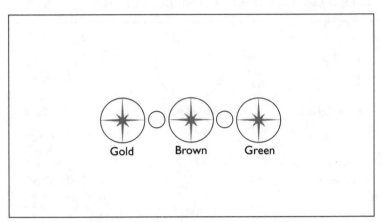

Fig. 3 Attract Money (See text, page 72.)

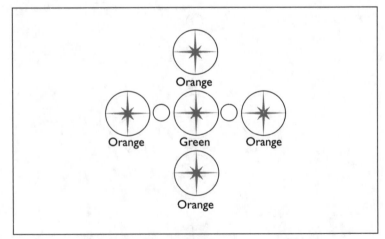

Fig. 4 Gain Prosperity (See text, page 73.)

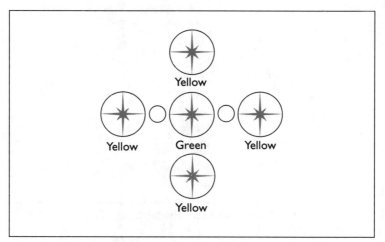

Fig. 5 Influence Someone to Repay a Debt (See text, page 74.)

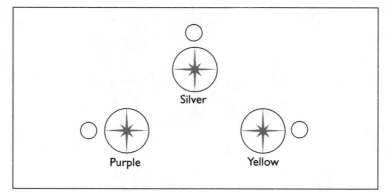

Fig. 6 Increase Personal Power (See text, page 76.)

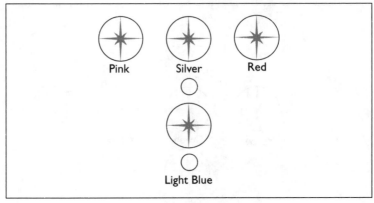

Fig. 7 Conquer Fear (See text, page 77.)

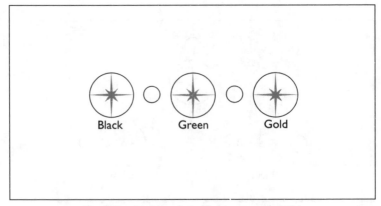

Fig. 8 Find a New Job (See text, page 78.)

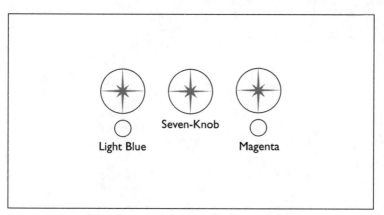

Fig. 9 Attain Success (See text, page 79.)

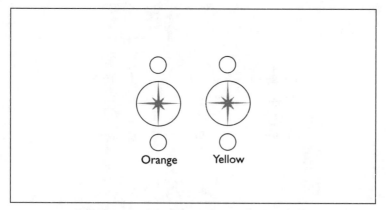

Fig. 10 Inspire Creativity (See text, page 80.)

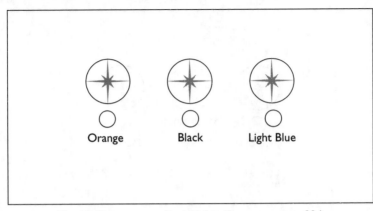

Fig. 11 Overcome a Bad Habit (See text, page 82.)

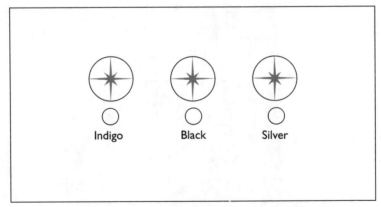

Fig. 12 Stop Arguments (See text, page 85.)

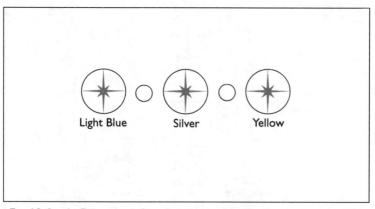

Fig. 13 Settle Disturbed Conditions in a Home (See text, page 84.)

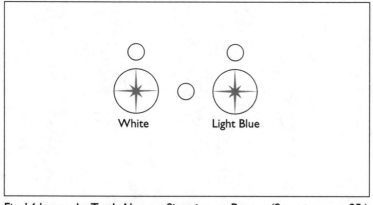

Fig. 14 Learn the Truth About a Situation or Person (See text, page 85.)

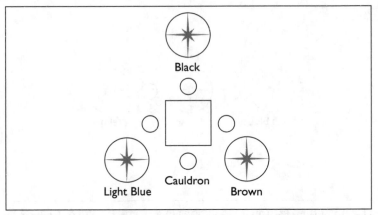

Fig. 15 Release Situations or People from Your Life (See text, page 86.)

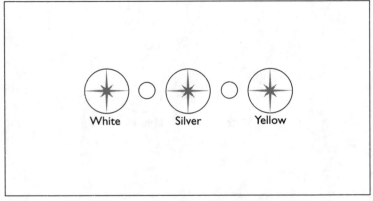

Fig. 16 Accept a Situation (See text, page 88.)

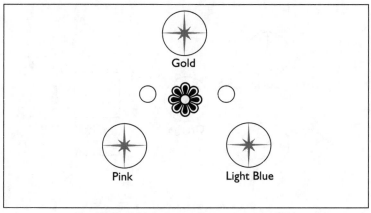

Fig. 17 Find Happiness (See text, page 89.)

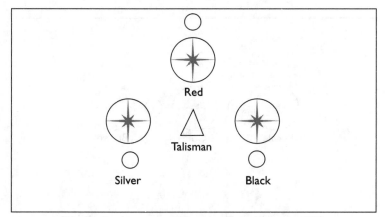

Fig. 18 Consecrate a Talisman (See text, page 90.)

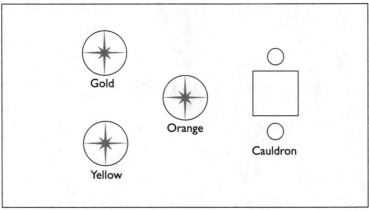

Fig. 19 Reach a Decision (See text, page 91.)

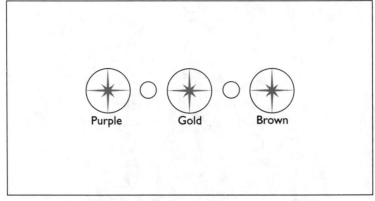

Fig. 20 Start a New Venture (See text, page 93.)

156

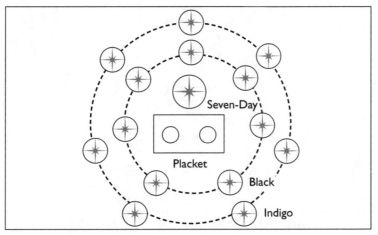

Fig. 21 Peaceful Divorce (See text, page 94.)

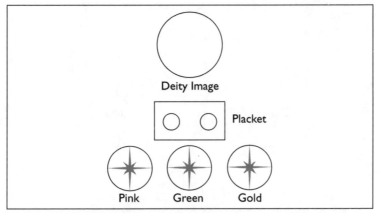

Fig. 22 Celebrate a Birth (See text, page 95.)

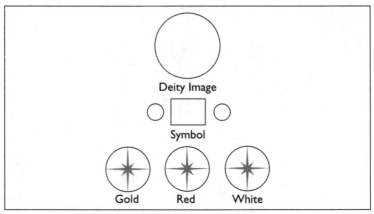

Fig. 23 Celebrate a Wedding Anniversary (See text, page 97.)

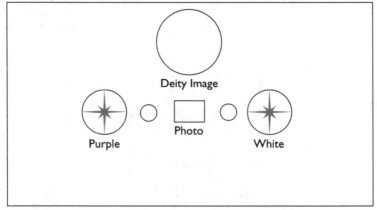

Fig. 24 In Memory of a Deceased Loved One (See text, page 98.)

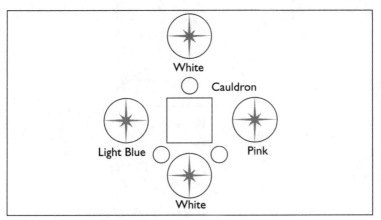

Fig. 25 Giving Thanks (See text, page 99.)

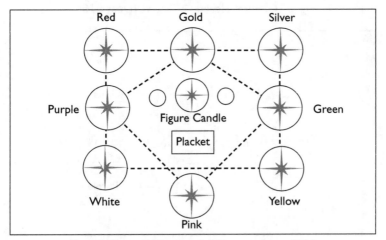

Fig. 26 General Healing 1 (See text, page 101.)

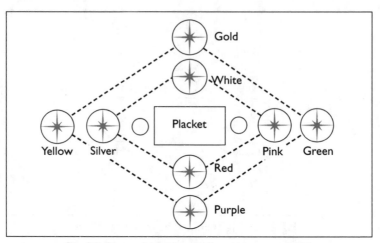

Fig. 27 General Healing 2 (See text, page 103.)

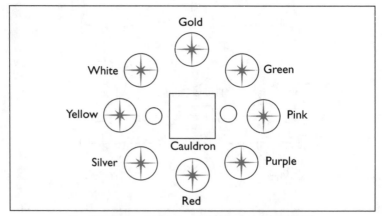

Fig. 28 General Healing 3 (See text, page 105.)

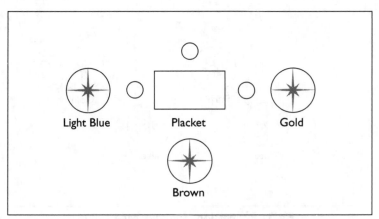

Fig. 29 Regain Health (See text, page 106.)

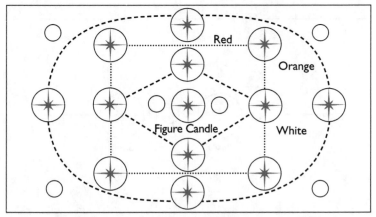

Fig. 30 Recover from Surgery (See text, page 107.)

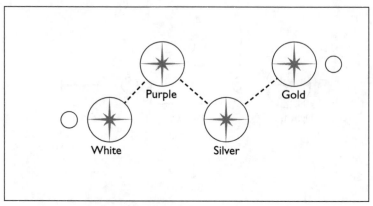

Fig. 31 Purification (See text, page 108.)

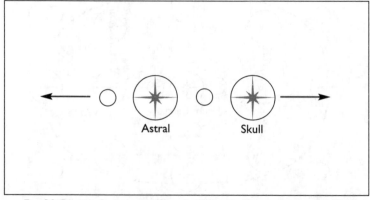

Fig. 32 Banish Serious or Terminal Illness (See text, page 110.)

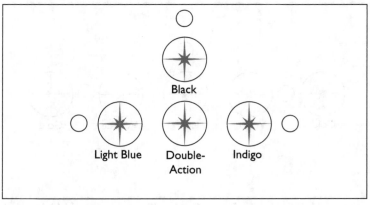

Fig. 33 Stop Interference in Your Love or Marriage (See text, page 112.)

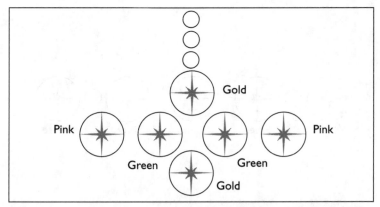

Fig. 34 Heal an Unhappy Marriage or Relationshi (See text, page 113.)

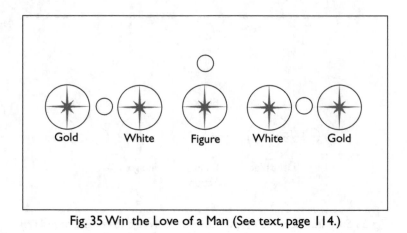

Fig. 35 Win the Love of a Man (See text, page 114.)

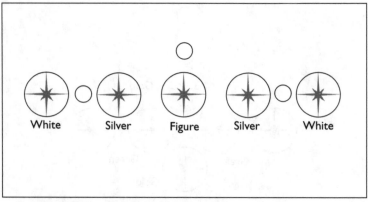

Fig. 36 Win the Love of a Woman (See text, page 115.)

164

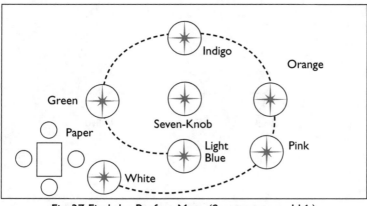

Fig. 37 Find the Perfect Mate (See text, page 116.)

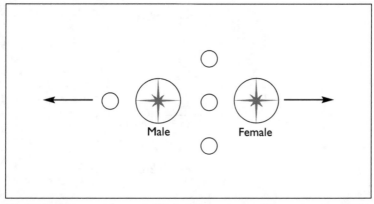

Fig. 38 Release an Unwanted Admirer or Lover (See text, page 118.)

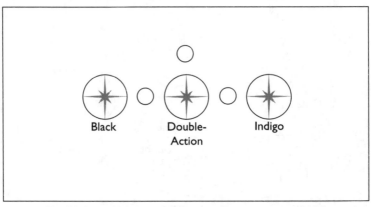

Fig. 39 Stop Slander and Gossip (See text, page 119.)

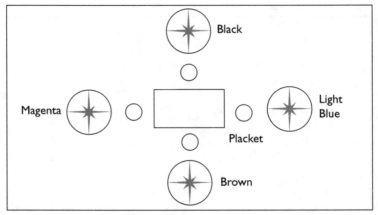

Fig. 40 Rid Yourself of Negatives (See text, page 121.)

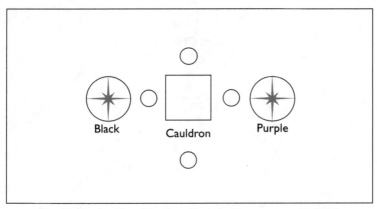

Fig. 41 Binding Troublesome People (See text, page 122.)

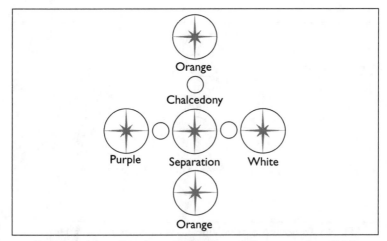

Fig. 42 Release One from Enthrallment (See text, page 123.)

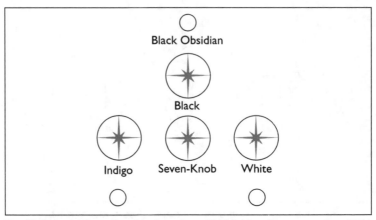

Fig. 43 Release from Psychic Attack or Ill-Wishing (See text, page 125.)

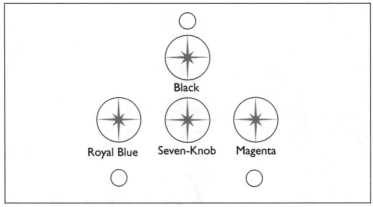

Fig. 44 Remove Negative Vibrations or Spirits from a Home
(See text, page 126.)

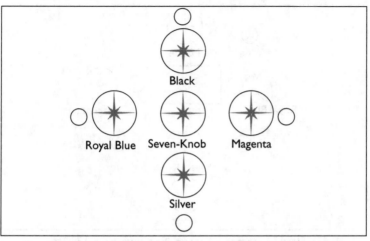

Fig. 45 Remove Negative Vibrations or Spirits from a Person
(See text, page 128.)

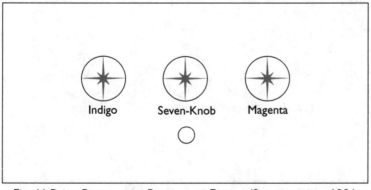

Fig. 46 Bring Pressure to Bear on an Enemy (See text, page 129.)

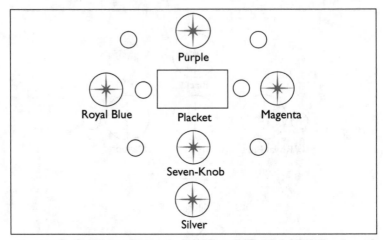

Fig. 47 Uncross a Person (See text, page 131.)

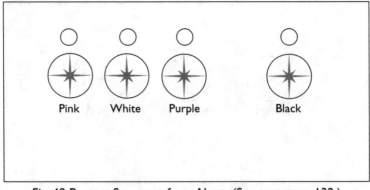

Fig. 48 Protect Someone from Abuse (See text, page 132.)

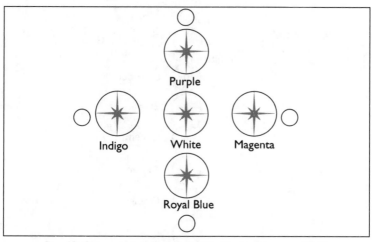

Fig. 49 Communicate with Spirit (See text, page 134.)

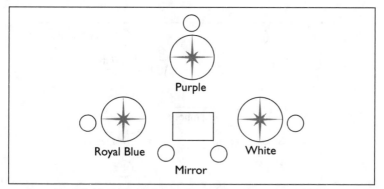

Fig. 50 Meet Your Spirit Guide (See text, page 135.)

171

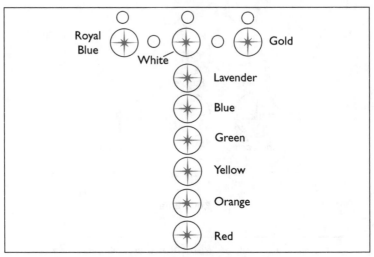

Fig. 51 Enhance Spiritual Growth (See text, page 137.)

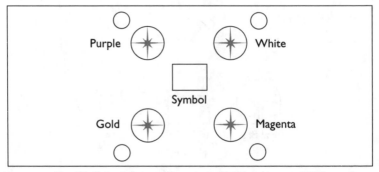

Fig. 52 Gain Spiritual Blessings (See text, page 138.)

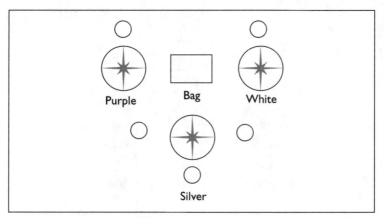

Fig. 53 Strengthen Your Psychic Abilities (See text, page 140.)

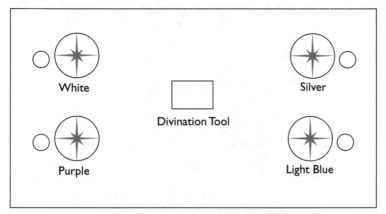

Fig. 54 Prepare for Divination (See text, page 141.)

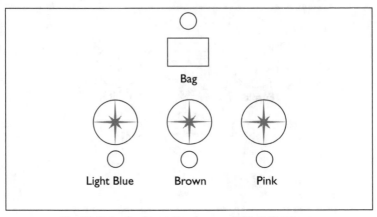

Fig. 55 Enhance Your Dreams and Find Guidance
(See text, page 143.)

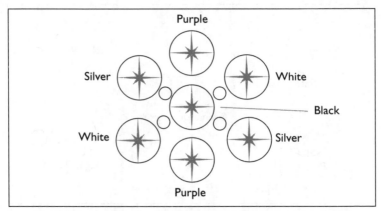

Fig. 56 Strengthen Your Psychic Shield (See text, page 144.)

Books by The Crossing Press

Other books by D.J. Conway

Crystal Enchantments:
A Complete Guide to Stones and Their Magical Properties

By D. J. Conway

D. J. Conway's book will help guide you in your choice of stones from Adularia to Zircon, by listing their physical properties and magical uses. It will also appeal to folks who are not into magic, but simply love stones and want to know more about them.

Paper • ISBN 1-58091-010-6

Laying on of Stones

By D. J. Conway

Stones can be used to protect and heal you, your family, and your home, but where to place them is often a source of difficulty. Probably the most important question frequently asked is where to place them on your body. D. J. Conway has supplied you with forty detailed diagrams, showing you exactly how to place a variety of stones to help your body heal itself of illness or enrich your life through a magical manifestation of desires.

Paper • ISBN 1-58091-029-7

Other books in the series

A Little Book of Love Magic

By Patricia Telesco

A cornucopia of lore, magic, and imaginative ritual designed to bring excitement and romance to your life. Patricia Telesco tells us how to use magic to manifest our hopes and dreams for romantic relationships, friendships, family relations, and passions for our work.

Paper • ISBN 0-89594-887-7

BOOKS BY THE CROSSING PRESS

Other books by Crossing

A Wisewoman's Guide to Spells, Rituals and Goddess Lore
By Elizabeth Brooke

A remarkable compendium of magical lore, psychic skills and women's mysteries.

Paper • ISBN 0-89594-779-X

All Women Are Healers:
A Comprehensive Guide to Natural Healing
By Diane Stein

Stein's bestselling book on natural healing for women teaches women to take control of their bodies and lives and offers a wealth of information on various healing methods including Reiki, Reflexology, Polarity Balancing, and Homeopathy.

Paper • ISBN 0-89594-409-X

Ariadne's Thread: A Workbook of Goddess Magic
By Shekinah Mountainwater

One of the finest books on women's spirituality available.—Sagewoman

Shekhinah Mountainwater's organized and well-written book encourages women to find their own spiritual path. This is a very good, practical book…recommended.—Library Journal

Paper • ISBN 0-89594-475-8

BOOKS BY THE CROSSING PRESS

Healing with the Energy of the Chakras

By Ambika Wauters

Chakras are swirling wheels of light and color—vortices through which energy must pass in order to nourish and maintain physical, emotional, mental and spiritual life. Wauters presents a self-help program intended to give you guidelines and a framework within which to explore and understand more about how your energetic system responds to thoughts and expression.

Paper • ISBN 0-89594-906-7

FutureTelling: A Complete Guide to Divination

By Patricia Telesco

This cross-cultural encyclopedia of divination practices gives over 250 entries, from simple signs and omens of traditional folk magic to complex rituals of oracular consultation.

Paper • ISBN 0-89594-872-9

Mother Wit: A Guide to Healing and Psychic Development

By Diane Mariechild

It is a joy to find this material from occult traditions and Eastern religions adapted by her woman-identified consciousness to the needs of women today.— Womanspirit

Paper • ISBN 0-89594-358-1

BOOKS BY THE CROSSING PRESS

Shamanism as a Spiritual Practice for Daily Life

By Tom Cowan

This inspirational book blends elements of shamanism with inherited traditions and contemporary religious commitments. An inspiring spiritual call.—Booklist

Paper • ISBN 0-89594-838-9

Spinning Spells, Weaving Wonders: Modern Magic for Everyday Life

By Patricia Telesco

This essential book of over 300 spells tells how to work with simple, easy-to-find components and focus creative energy to meet daily challenges with awareness, confidence, and humor.

Paper • ISBN 0-89594-803-6

The Wiccan Path: A Guide for the Solitary Practitioner

By Rae Beth

This is a guide to the ancient path of the village wisewoman. Writing in the form of letters to two apprentices, Rae Beth provides rituals for the key festivals of the wiccan calendar. She also describes the therapeutic powers of trancework and herbalism, and outlines the Pagan approach to finding a partner.

Paper • ISBN 0-89594-744-7

For a current catalog of books from The Crossing Press
visit our Web site: **www.crossingpress.com**